Sickness and Healing

Biblical Encounters Series

Suffering by Erhard S. Gerstenberger and Wolfgang Schrage
translated by John E. Steely
Festival and Joy by Eckhart Otto and Tim Schramm
translated by James L. Blevins
World and Environment by Odil Hannes Steck
Death and Life by Otto Kaiser and Eduard Lohse
translated by John E. Steely
Faith by Hans-Jürgen Hermisson and Eduard Lohse
translated by Douglas Stott
Achievement by Antonius H. J. Gunneweg
and Walter Schmithals
translated by David Smith
Time and History by Siegfried Herrmann
translated by James L. Blevins

Sickness and Healing

Klaus Seybold
and
Ulrich B. Mueller

Biblical Encounters Series

Translated by Douglas W. Stott

ABINGDON
Nashville

KRANKHEIT UND HEILUNG

© 1978 Verlag W. Kohlhammer GmbH

SICKNESS AND HEALING

Translation copyright © 1981 by Abingdon

Library of Congress Cataloging in Publication Data

SEYBOLD, KLAUS.
  Sickness and healing.
  (Biblical encounters series)
  Translation of: Krankheit und Heilung.
  Bibliography: p.
  1. Healing in the Bible. 2. Medicine in the Bible. I. Mueller, Ulrich B. II.
  Title. III. Series.
  BS680.H4S4913   233'.5   81-3663   AACR2
        ISBN 0-687-38444-3

Scripture quotations are from the Revised Standard Version of the Bible,
copyrighted 1946, 1952, © 1971, 1973 by the Division of Christian Education of
the National Council of the Churches of Christ in the U.S.A., and are used by
permission.

MANUFACTURED BY THE PARTHENON PRESS AT
NASHVILLE, TENNESSEE, UNITED STATES OF AMERICA

Contents

CONTENTS

CONTENTS

Introduction: Sickness as Problem and as Motif in the Biblical Tradition

If one wishes to discover what the biblical tradition has to say about the problem of sickness, one must first become aware of several difficulties that blur any direct access to the motif.

One must first recognize that our understanding of the word "sick," of who is really sick, and what sickness really is, is to a large extent—and quite decisively—determined by the view of life and man our own age holds; that understanding is also historically conditioned, indeed in part by precisely the value system of the biblical tradition. That means our understanding is relative, and that relativity only emerges with a historical comparison. To that extent, then, one's understanding of sickness and health as that particular balance constituting life is always dependent upon much more comprehensive reference systems. Nonetheless, our own understanding, nourished and supported by continually new experiences, has a security that at least demands our willingness to open up to examples of the same or similar life experiences.

In the second place, one must remember that the definition of the term "sickness" offered by the science of medicine has achieved its revolutionary successes, above all, but not exclusively, by means of diagnostic processes—an ever more precise and exhaustive understanding of individual manifestations of sickness. However, the understanding of just what all these variations and forms of sickness have in common has by no means kept pace with those diagnostic successes. Indeed, in some quarters one hears the opinion that this kind of precise theoretical definition of sickness as a life process and individual vital procedure is not possible at all. Instead, we have academic interpretations, various images or ideas which are sometimes determined more scientifically according to physical and chemical processes, and sometimes more psychosomatically according to social forces and reactions. They all orient themselves to the same given model, but their lack of unity and their sheer scope considerably influence the pre- and extra-scientific conceptions of sickness that abound in our time and society.

In the third place, one must remember that sickness is dependent upon the life situation itself; like all human things, it, too, has a history. Sicknesses emerge, proliferate, gain hold, and then die out. There are both old and young diseases. Antiquity did not know all the diseases of modern times, and similarly not all diseases of antiquity—particularly epidemics—are extant today.

In the fourth place—and this summarizes all our previous points—just as in all historical considerations, the historical distance from the speakers of the biblical tradition and the linguistic, mental, and social differences impede any direct access to the statements, accounts, or interpretations of sickness and to the medical texts. This can be further aggravated by the vagueness or lack of clarity of the statement itself. Thus the Hebrew terms *ḥalā* or *ḥolî*—examples from the Old Testament—cannot simply be translated as "to become sick" or "to be sick," or as "sickness" in general, since their field of meaning is larger than that of our terms. It encompasses bodily weakness in general—as one can see in the example of Samson, who when his hair was cut off, lost his superhuman strength and "became weak, and was like any other man" (Judg. 16:7, 11, 13). Similarly, the difficulties in rendering the Hebrew term *ṣara ' at* are enormous, and in their own way are paradigmatic for the terrain awaiting us here. The word means "wasp sting" and had become the symptomatic designation of various skin diseases which were difficult to define, though in part generally quite harmless (harmless for us; antiquity had other standards). They hardly, however, included the disease known today as leprosy. The translations of this term became pathological themselves and precipitated a history of suffering without equal. In Greek one said *lepra*, which means "leprosy" in English (German *Aussatz*). This lack of real differentiation, along with the supposed biblical sanction, made "lepers" out of many of the sick people. One must thus be extremely careful with the biblical terminology, accounts, and diagnoses referring to sickness or disease. Any direct path is full of danger.

Because of that danger, this presentation cannot be prefaced by any firmly outlined and fixed concept of sickness, no matter what kind. One should look rather for a preliminary definition of the term, or better, for a heuristic model whose constitutive elements can be described phenomenologically. Its search mechanism should be flexible enough to adapt to the various appearances and should, at the same time, be capable of showing us to what extent we are dealing with what we call "sickness." Such a heuristic model would have to include the following points. The phenomonology of sickness and disease[1] suggests

1. that it is experienced and described as a physical and pyschological reality by the individual person in pain and life diminution;
2. that some kind of therapeutic effort is put into motion as a reaction; its apparatus is normally prepared by medical science or its antecedents, and its goal is healing as the reestablishment of the previous condition. The sick person assumes the role of patient;
3. that the end of life—death as the limit of life—becomes visible, and that sickness or disease appears as a crisis in life;
4. that the question arises concerning the meaning of this crisis, situation, or event, precipitating—in the persons concerned—diagnoses, interpretations, theories, and other remarks concerning the situation at hand.

These criteria offer a method of differentiating this understanding of sickness from similar anthropological phenomena, such as suffering, death, or societal sicknesses, to which some of the points do not apply. Nonetheless, the boundaries are in many cases quite fluid. This definition simultaneously suggests another, different dimensional model. K. E. Rothschuh[2] has suggested that sickness be defined within the context of the persons (or groups) affected, and to whom the sickness appears in various aspects. This yields a framelike pyramid relationship showing us that sickness manifests itself for the sick person as a situation needing assistance *(aegritudo)*, as a sense of being sick; and for the physician as a clinical phenomenon, a substratum and example of sickness *(nosos, pathos);* and finally, for the compassionate societal members, as an emergency situation *(infirmitas)* which must be given aid. "Sickness thus appears in different contexts (relationships, applicable situations) in spite of fundamental identity. The various perspectives allow different aspects of sickness to come into the foreground. This means that something quite different can be meant by the word 'sickness' in spite of the use of the same word, and it explains why various understandings of 'sickness' are possible."[3] Rothschuh offers the following conceptual definition:

> "A person is sick who becomes subjectively and/or clinically and/or socially in need of help as a result of losing the balanced cooperation of the physical or psychological or psycho-physical functional parts of the organism. . . . Sickness is then the situation of the subjective and/or clinical and/or social need for help of a person resulting from the loss of the balanced cooperation among the physical, psychological or psycho-physical functional parts of the organism.

This scheme could be further refined, the pyramid structure further expanded, but since we need a heuristic model with a very basic standard of measurement, and since we want to focus the model—in accordance with our whole realm of concern—on (biblical) texts from antiquity, the relational model must be modified.

Sickness also prompts—particularly within the biblical tradition—in all three pyramidal instances (sick person, physician, society), the question of how a phenomenon seen so variously can be ordered into the larger framework of human life and world reality. How does it fit into the larger and largest contexts of existence, i.e., what is its meaning?[4] Since the biblical tradition brings in a dimension one can call the religious side of the matter, or the theological relation, that model appears to be in need of revision for our purposes so that the vertical dimension of sickness in the view of the persons concerned can come to light.

This kind of scheme—broken down according to individual feeling, social involvement and concern, and religious challenge—will function in a guiding fashion in the following presentation, explicitly and implicitly in both sections. We hope that in this way justice is done both to the very real character of sickness on the one hand, and to the intention of the biblical passages on the other.

The Old Testament section offers first a presentation of the situation of the sick person within the course of Israelite history and within the milieu of the Near-Eastern environment (I). This is followed by a presentation of the statements concerning sickness and disease in the individual literary layers and writings (II). Next, several cases of sickness are treated separately (the "leprosy" of Saul, Ezekiel, the Suffering Servant, Job) (III). A summary attempts to draw the anthropological conclusions from the Old Testament development (IV), and a glance forward follows the lines in the later period up to the doorstep of the New Testament.[5]

A.
OLD TESTAMENT

I. The Situation of the Sick Person in Israel and Its Near-Eastern Environment: Framework and Background

The foundation and framework of our presentation of Old Testament statements about sickness and healing will be a brief description of the situation in which the sick person in ancient Israel found himself. Since this situation is best illuminated by the statements, designations, and descriptions of those actually affected, we will first make a few remarks concerning the linguistic forms in which they are expressed.

1. Language

Anyone in ancient Israel wanting to describe a weakened condition accompanied by pain, in words going beyond the universally human, elementary, and spontaneous forms of expression such as "ah!" and "woe!" or "oh, my head, my head!" (2 Kings 4:19), would use the word *ḥalā* (verb), meaning "to be weak or sick," or its derivations. The same thing holds true for becoming healthy again. Here the word *rafa* (verb), "to make whole," indicated the reestablishment of health. Derived from it is the relatively rare Old Testament designation for "physician," or better, "surgeon, assistant medical officer" (*rofe* , participle, actually meaning "one who makes whole"). Clustered around these terms is a limited number of other terms which, on the one hand, emphasize more the feeling of pain, and, on the other, more the external condition. There is a special word for the condition of discomfort of the women (*dawäh*), which, to be sure, is often figuratively used to refer to the condition of the "heart" (*leb*). This is also the case outside the Old Testament on an ostrakon from Lachis 3:7 (6th century).[6]

The lack of sharpness in these statements is not really the

noteworthy element here; this can hardly be surprising in daily language or folk poetry. What is striking is rather the sobriety and clarity with which one deals here with sickness—one might even say in a technical, distanced, or objective fashion. This is apparent in the use of the verb "to make whole," which can also refer to the mending, for example, of a clay pot (Jer. 19:11); the same holds true for the technically determined "to be sick or weak." Whereas the entire Semitic world used a word of common etymology to designate the condition of sickness, that other word—as we see from the Old Testament—asserted itself in ancient Israel (the Old Testament does use the common Semitic word in some passages in the Hebrew form mrṣ, but it displays a much more dark, even obscure, meaning in the sense of "to be bad or ruinous"). This word, however, according to its etymology and history, probably originally had the technical meaning "rust," "to become rusty."[7] Even Ecclesiastes appears to want to play on this echo when he speaks of the sore affliction inherent in the fact that God does not give a man the power to enjoy his wealth and possessions—similar to the destructive rust (6:1-2).

In ancient Israel there were thus forces capable of suppressing the unpleasant associations of sickness in favor of a more objective view—to the extent that this can be said on the basis of the writings chosen from the Old Testament. Since these forces, as will be seen, cannot be traced back to the largely peripheral influence in ancient Israel of the art of healing or medical science, and since they also cannot have any connection with the Near-Eastern Wisdom movement (this would not explain the peculiar behavior here), only religious questions can be considered. An obvious assumption appears to be that this linguistic behavior was a consequence of the tight connection obtaining theologically between sickness and the will of Yahweh, a connection freeing the phenomenon for an objective treatment and understanding.

Two characteristics attract our attention in the actual designations and names of sicknesses. We notice first the relative frequency of words formed from terms meaning "to hit or strike"; secondly we find the special linguistic structure for the names of sicknesses, namely a feminine noun form (*qaṭṭalat*, e.g. "the slinking one," "glowing one," "burning one" and so on—all feminine designations, as well as *ṣara ' at*, "the one like a wasp sting,"[8] normally rendered as "leprosy"). Both peculiarities allude to half-conscious, rather vague images or ideas. The idea of "hitting" points to external causes (analogous to wounds). The imagery of the hand of God, also used frequently in Israel, belongs in this context, a hand which strikes or weighs heavily upon a person.[9] The typical noun form uncovers older, dynamistic views which only occasionally—and then in more graphic-poetic speech—still play a role in Old Testament literature.

The transition to peculiarly medicinal terminology is fluid. We find an attempt at the diagnostic differentiation of skin diseases only in Leviticus 13–15, significantly in sacral, medicinal instructions for evaluating the cultic purity of the priest's hand. Otherwise it is interesting that two areas find particularly frequent expression in Old Testament writings: the areas of sex and age. Various manifestations, such as the sterility of a woman, or sexual emissions, and also the appearance of aging, are considered sickness in the sense of bodily weakness. On the whole, one can say that more precise descriptions of an understanding of sickness appear only in the later period of the Old Testament, and that even then the views of folk medicine dominate. As one example among several (such as Ps. 38, Ps. 107:17-20), let us look at the late syndrome description of a typical case of sickness (which is in other ways generally significant), Job 33:19-22: "Man is also chastened with pain upon his bed, and with continual strife in his bones; so that his life loaths bread, and his appetite dainty food. His flesh is so wasted away that it cannot be seen; and his bones which were not seen stick out. His soul draws near the Pit. . . ." As we said, it is a typical description. It does not try to give a diagnosis in the sense of a precise description of the symptoms, but seeks rather to emphasize and characterize the situation of the sick person in a way distinguishing it from other life situations and crises (Ps. 107). From this kind of situational analysis the description then wants to discover guidelines for corresponding behavior. The description of the situation merges here with the determination of the role the sick person is to assume.

2. Role

In ancient Israel, a sick person found himself placed in a role that determined both his reactions and his behavior beyond normal individual and concrete circumstances. Two examples with essentially paradigmatic significance can demonstrate this. "When a man has on the skin of his body a swelling or an eruption or a spot, and it turns into leprous disease on the skin of his body, then he shall be brought to Aaron the priest . . . and he shall pronounce him unclean." This excerpt comes from the beginning of the so-called leprosy-Torah (instruction concerning ṣara ' at) in Leviticus 13–14, and is transmitted in a relatively late stratum of the so-called Priestly writing; it shows there was a "legal" procedure calling for the employment of a priest whenever one suspected "leprosy" in the sense of the definition given there. The priest would then decide, on the basis of diagnostic examinations that were quite difficult to carry out, whether the case was indeed "leprosy." His decision was not to serve as a basis for therapy in a medical sense, but was rather to determine purity or impurity in a cultic sense. It resulted in exclusion from the worship service assembly, and beyond that, from the life community in general. The person sick with "leprosy" was excluded until healed and purified. The Torah prescribes: "The leper who has the disease shall wear torn clothes and let the hair of his head hang loose, and he shall cover his upper lip and cry, 'Unclean, unclean.' He shall remain unclean as long as he has the disease; he is unclean; he shall dwell alone in a habitation outside the camp" (Lev. 13:45 f). The concept of the "camp" here is characterized by the priestly theology and alludes to the sacral idea of the proper form of existence of a "pure" community. However, comparatively old as well as later texts show that "lepers" were given the role of "excluded persons" in practice as well (Num. 12; 2 Kings 5 and 15; Deut. 24:8 and Luke 17:11-19 [B. III.]). The ancient oriental mind considered skin diseases to be particularly serious because of their visible manifestations.

The second example is Job. In the Book of Job his case counts as a paradigm of the sick person. It is not clear, however, whether his case is understood to be "leprosy." In any case, the term ṣara ' at does not appear in the book. It is quite certain, however, that each section of the work is concerned with proper behavior in the face of sickness, and thus, primarily, with the role of the sick person. We are told that Job at first submitted to the demands of the role. Just as the "leper's" appearance shows, by means of penitence or self-debasement rites, that he knows himself to be in the condition of someone struck or affected, so also does Job react in the customary manner: he sits among the ashes as a penitent. His friends go through the normal procedure of grief: weeping, rending robes, sprinkling of dust upon their heads toward heaven; and to all this, there no doubt also belonged a period of fixed silence before the lament breaks out.[10]

Otherwise, however, one does not learn a great deal from the Old Testament concerning the social status of the sick person. The example of Job, as well as the many (unfortunately, often obscure) laments of sick people in the psalms that refer to enemies and persecutors, suggests this was an extremely dark chapter in ancient Israel and that the material (work disability) as well as religious consequences (divine punishment) very often weighed heavily upon the person concerned. Perhaps the "genre image" portrayed in Job 19 shows us some of the social misery in which the sick person found himself. It is an image of social perversion; all the normal community relationships are turned upside down and transformed into their exact opposite:

He has put my brethren far from me, and my acquaintances are wholly estranged from me. My kinsfolk and my close friends have failed me; the guests in my house have forgotten me; my maidservants count me as a stranger; I have become an alien in their eyes. I call to my servant, but he gives me no answer; I must beseech him with my mouth. I am repulsive to my wife, loathesome to the sons of my own mother. Even young children despise me; when I rise they talk against me. All my intimate friends abhor me, and those whom I loved

have turned against me. My bones cleave to my skin and to my
flesh, and I have escaped by the skin of my teeth. Have pity on
me, have pity on me, O you my friends, for the hand of God has
touched me! Why do you, like God, pursue me? Why are you
not satisfied with my flesh? (Job 19:13-22; see below chap. II, 2)

3. Institutions

According to 2 Kings 15:5, the "leprous" king Uzziah lived
in a special house called a *bêt haḥāfšît*, while his son took care of
governmental business. If this designation is to be rendered "bed
house, infirmary" (or "house of freedom," euphemistically
meaning "lack of freedom"—in Ugaritic a similar designation is
used to refer to the underworld) then we would have here a
reference (admittedly singular) to the existence of a kind of
"hospital" in Israel. However, we must simultaneously add that
this is a matter of the privilege of a king; this house was, no doubt,
not for the general public. Otherwise we hear nothing in the Old
Testament about public institutions serving health matters. In all
probability there were no such institutions in ancient Israel. In
addition, previous archaeological discoveries from the daily life
of the iron-age Palestinian area do not allow us to speak about
general hygienic institutions.[11] Physicians play a role only in the
later period; other institutions took over whatever health care
one can speak of at all.

For information one turned to the oracles, the holy places,
and the prophets (again primarily used only by kings), and
occasionally to foreign authorities such as Baalzebub in Philistine
Ekron (2 Kings 1), normally—as we see from the narratives—
with the question concerning the alternatives, life or death.

One could then, of course, seek help in the extensive
medicinal black market, which we may describe with catch-
phrases such as conjuring and magic and which in the Old
Testament is known to us primarily in the negative image of
polemic; here one no longer let the Yahweh faith be the
determining factor, but rather put all hope in the divine
physician. The severity of the disputes ignited by this question

shows us that this sort of offer represented a continual temptation for Israel, for example in Ezekiel 13:17-23, the accusation against false prophetesses. They are accused of manipulating dying or sick people by means of "magic bands" and "veils for the head"—procedures quite similar to Babylonian incantations.[12] On the other hand, people remained aware that they had to distinguish themselves in these matters from procedures customary elsewhere. In a way seldom found in the Old Testament, the story of Naaman in 2 Kings 5 tells us which temptations and unreasonable expectations confronted Israel from other quarters: "Behold, I thought that he would surely come out to me, and stand, and call on the name of the Lord his God, and wave his hand over the place, and cure the leper" (v 11).

Israel's faith offered the sick person only one alternative: prayer as a confession and entreaty for healing, together with the normal penitential rites. In many cases these were no doubt presided over by a priest (Job 33:23 f). The healed person had the opportunity to be restored cultically and socially by means of purification rites and atonement, and by means of celebrations enhancing the feeling of community. This amounted to the attainment of a rehabilitated status, tailored, as it were, to antiquity's understanding of sickness.[13]

4. The Medical Arts

We know practically nothing about ancient Israelite medicine. The trepanned skulls found in Lachis—in spite, or even because, of their singularity—by no means imply an "advanced stage of medicinal art in Judea during the time of the prophet Isaiah,"[14] since trepanation is an achievement of stone-age culture; furthermore, in this case it could well have been practiced by the Assyrian medical officers. What the Old Testament offers us in the way of occasional medical terminology (or what we consider to be such terminology), or healing procedures, does not really suffice to give us a clear picture. At any rate, references to "cakes of fig" (Isa. 38:21) or the specialized expression "food for the sick" (2 Sam. 13:5, 7, 10, perhaps also Ps. 69:21) lead us to conclude—if one can conclude anything here at all—that we cannot expect much beyond folk medicine. It may very well be, of course, that the Old Testament accounts are one-sidedly biased for the purpose of denigrating medicinal healing practices; but it is nonetheless noticeable that not even a trace can be found in Israel of that kind of medicine which was, to a certain extent, so highly developed and specialized in the Fertile Crescent as well as in Egypt. Are we to take this as the result of the Yahweh religion, which was so critical of medicinal practices, particularly since virtually all our efforts seem to point us in the direction of sacramental diagnoses (Lev. 13-15)? The late remark chastising one for turning to the physicians instead of Yahweh in the case of foot trouble (2 Chron. 16:12), and the extensive argumentation with which Sirach 38 must try to justify the medical arts, both show that this was, and remained, a problem: "Honor the physician with the honor due him, according to your need of him, for the Lord created him; for healing comes from the Most High, and he will receive a gift from the king" (vv 1 f). The religious claim associated with all healing practices in antiquity was no doubt the reason behind the Yahweh religion's opposition.

The ancient Israelite sick person was thus not able to expect help from common medicinal practice. Accordingly, knowledge of physiology was in general at a comparatively low level. If we collect the manifold and disparate examples offered by the Old Testament, we get a very typical overall picture.[15] There are, to be sure, designations for external bodily parts; but concerning "the internal parts of the body" we find only extremely vague and inexact ideas. They speak about the rump, the heart, the body, and viscera, more symbolically and metaphorically about the "innermost parts" (Prov. 20:27) and the genitals, they know about the liver for particular reasons (the prophetic viewing of an animal's liver), the kidneys (seat of the conscience?) and—only in Job—about the "gall" (16:13), but apparently know nothing about their organic functions. The Old Testament completely lacks any terms for lungs, stomach, and intestines. There is not one unambiguous example suggesting that sickness or disease were associated with one of the organs, or even with internal parts of the body. Sickness was viewed as blows or attacks by a higher power in analogy to bodily wounds. There simply are no other etiologies in the Old Testament.

The situation of the sick person—if one were to summarize this information—was characterized by opacity, helplessness, and insecurity; sickness was a deep and serious life crisis. This is why the lament psalms view the sick person as being in close proximity to the underworld: at the gates of Sheol, or already in the realm of death. If he gets well again, one speaks about becoming alive, about a return to the light of life. It was considered an act of God, and a miracle.[16]

Two things prompt us now to take a look at Israel's ancient Near-Eastern environment. First, we wish to illustrate the sick person's situation in Israel by means of texts outside the Old Testament that come from comparable, historically related cultural epochs, particularly texts that came up short or were suppressed during the Old Testament canonization process. This discussion primarily concerns the day-to-day situation of the sick person with its religious and quasi-religious substructure. Second, this presentation of the ancient oriental background serves to throw the Israelite scene into sharper relief within the light of its environment, and enables us to determine which function is to be attributed to the Old Testament examples in this area. It goes without saying that this can only be a very fragmentary sketch, not least because of the lack of sufficient source material; furthermore, what material we do have available has not yet been evaluated specifically for the purpose of portraying the situation of the sick person.

5. The Canaanite Environment

It is totally impossible to reconstruct the role of sickness and disease within the pre-Israelite or extra-Israelite Caananite cultural arena, including the Philistine and Phoenician cities. The sparse and sporadic information and archaelogical finds offer no unified picture at all. In the north Syrian town of Arslan Tasch (Chadattu) (seventh century) an amulet has been found with incantations against night demons and evil eyes, composed in a Phoenician-Aramaic dialect and to a large extent still undeciphered. This amulet has, among others, an incantation of Chavron, a Canaanite god also conjured in a Ugaritic text, whose name is still preserved in the name of the city Bet-Horon (bēt 'ur)[17], where he no doubt had his sanctuary.[18] Then there is also the Akkadian incantation against the fever demon Lamaschtu from Ugarit.[19] Large numbers of amulets with pictorial symbols and without accompanying writing have also been found, and with these we can compare allusions in the Old Testament such as that in 1 Samuel 6:4. According to 2 Kings 1, the god of the Philistine city Ekron, Baalzebub, appears to have been a "medicinal" authority—in the sense of an oracle—who was known beyond the boundaries of his own city. Reschef, the god of the underworld, of epidemics, and of war in the Ugaritic pantheon, appears to have played a role in the entire Phoenician-Canaanite realm. The Old Testament has also preserved allusions to the god of the plague (Ps. 78:48, also Hab. 3:5 and Job 5:7).[20] The old place name Rašpunna, in Greek, Apollonia (Arabic 'arsūf in Herzlija) recalls this god.[21]

For the rest, the Mesopotamian-Egyptian portrayal of the sick person's external situation—something we will present later—probably corresponded with fair accuracy to the reality of ancient Canaanite daily life. Perhaps we can attribute a more universal significance to a passage in the Ugaritic KRT-epic, even though it is concerned with a king's illness, for whom—as was the case for King Ahaziah in Israel (2 Kings 1)—more alternatives were available than for the common person. After King KRT became sick, after pain became the "sister of his bed and sickness the wife of his bed," El, the highest and most powerful of all the gods, asks help from the assembly of the gods seven times. When this comes to nothing, El can only seek refuge in magic and incantation. It succeeds, however, and KRT is restored to health.[22]

An image preserved on a clay tablet in Ugarit is illustrative of Canaanite daily life.[23] An oracle is brought in when a child becomes sick. The oracle itself issues from the "Lord of the great gods" and comes to a mediator named *Dtn* with instructions for a magical procedure. Among other things, a figurine, either of the sick child or of the sickness demon(?), is to be prepared, taken to the temple and stamped to dust there, since "that is his sickness" *(ḥlh.w).* Furthermore, a messenger is to pick up the oracle— probably in written form—from *Dtn.* This oracle also appears on the clay tablet as a kind of protocol comment from *Dtn.* It reads:

> Dash the figurine to pieces,
> neither fish nor bread
> and afterwards no bitterness!

Perhaps one can interpret it such that the first line refers to the magical rite performed on the figurine, the second to medicinal dietary advice, and the third—even if vaguely—to the prognosis suggesting that only after this kind of treatment can one expect an end to the suffering *(mr).* This is a procedure that is typical in its interweaving of cultic-magical and practical-medicinal aspects.

From the Amarna period we have a letter from Rib-Addis of Byblos to the Pharaoh, written during a stopover in Beirut while a revolt was going on in Byblos. The writer complains that sickness and aging are plaguing him with all sorts of unpleasantries, the sickness accompanied by the implications, apparently customary there as well, of penitential rites, which in his position could no doubt have political consequences. He writes: "I am ancient of days, and my body has a heavy pain *(murzu dannu).* And may the King, my Lord, know that the gods of Gubla (Byblos) are *angered,* and that the pain is very grievous *(as a result of that),* and that I have confessed my sins *(ḫieti)* to the gods. In such circumstances I have not come before the King, my Lord."[24]

There is then another letter from King Niqmad to Pharaoh Amenophis IV throwing significant light on the plight of the sick person even in the rich city of Ugarit: "May my Lord give me two Nubian court pages, and give me a palace physician! There is no physician here!"[25] An Egyptian grave relief (fifteenth century) from the life of the physician Neb-Amon corresponds to this image; it portrays a dignified Syrian as a patient who has set out by ship and oxcart—similar to Naaman (2 Kings 5)—in order to be healed by the famous Egyptian physicians.[26]

6. Mesopotamia

The situation of the sick person in the Fertile Crescent appears to be characterized by two factors that, according to A. L. Oppenheim, can be traced back to the development of two medicinal traditions: a theoretical and a practical one. Both directions collected their knowledge into tablet series, the omen texts and the medicine texts; both had centers and both were carried on by experts, the incantation priest (āšipu) and the practical physician (asû). Both institutions appear to have been accessible to the general public to a large degree, though the latter occupied the weaker position, which resulted in a gradual decline in practical healing procedures and medicine over a period of time.[27]

The examination and treatment of a sick person by a practical physician was a possibility at least in the court and in cities. In all probability, however, this did not happen as described by Herodotus, who suggests that the Babylonians carried their sick to the market place and there displayed them to passers-by for examination (Babiloniaca III, 1). Perhaps the practical physician identified a malady according to his list of symptoms ("If someone is sick with . . . , or is suffering with . . . ") and adjusted the treatment according to the appropriate prescription. The variously praised surgical procedures (cataract operation, Caesarean section) prove—upon closer investigation—to be folk-medicine procedures also known elsewhere. Eye operations according to the Code of Hammurabi (218) are actually only relief incisions, and the frequently mentioned, highly praised Caesarean section was performed on the mother after she was already dead. Both complaints and praise of physicians are expressed in letters of the time.

The manipulations of the incantation priest have often been

described and are well-known,[28] and they presuppose a religious understanding of sickness. The healing itself is based on the magical effect of exorcism, and there are many examples of prayers to the deity also accompanying the rites. A large part of Akkadian prayer literature comes from this kind of *Sitz im Leben*. As an example, we can cite an epistolary incantation instruction which also offers a commentary on the famous picture of an incantation scene during an illness. This picture appears on a bronze tablet used as an amulet (reproduction on p. 29).

"As regards the ceremonies [during] the incantation 'You are the evil one,' about which my Lord King has written me—[namely] in order to exorcize the evil *alū* [i.e. sickness demon] and the fever attack [?]—one should perform rites as [one performs them during] what[ever] attacks the body; the incantation priest should come . . . [an animal], a young plant should be hung up on the gate beams [?], the conjurer should clothe himself with a red garment, a . . . should be summoned, . . . [a raven], [in] his ri[ght], a falcon [in his left hand] . . . he should strike with a whip . . . he should recite the incantation 'you are the evil one' . . . he should let the incense container, the torch surround them at the sides of (?) the bed of the sick one, to the gate he should recite the incantation '*hulduppū* depart,' he should conjure the door until they [the demons] depart; in the morning [and] in the evening he should act [in this way]."[29]

The "incantation against toothache" shows how this kind of incantation sounds:

> After Anu [created the heaven],
> and heaven created [the earth],
> and the earth created the rivers,
> and the rivers created the trenches,
> and the trenches created the quagmire,
> and the quagmire had created the worm,
> the worm went weeping before Shamash (sun god),
> before Ea (water god) his tears flow
> "What do you give (me) for my food?
> What do you give (me) so that I suck it?"

Assyrian bronze tablet, beginning of the millenium, height 13.5 cm (Collection Clercq, Paris). Compare AOB Nr. 387, ANEP Nr. 658. As in O. Keel, *Die Welt der altorientalischen Bildsymbolik und das AT*, 2nd edition 1977, p. 69, Nr. 91/92. Copyright Benziger Verlag, Zürich, Köln, 1972, used with permission.[30]

"I will give you a ripe fig (?), a
pomegranate (?), and an apple!"
"What am I to do with a ripe fig (?), a
pomegranate (?) and an apple?
Raise me up and let me live between the teeth
  and the gums (?)!
Let me suck out the blood of the teeth!
And let me devour the teeth flesh (?), teeth roots (?)!"
Make the lock bolt secure!
Because you have said such things, O worm,
may Ea strike you down with his strong hand!

Incantation against toothache
Treatment for it: Foul mix-beer mix together with oil
thrice say the incantation over it and
lay (it) upon his (the sick person's) tooth[31]

The complex treatment corresponds to the assumed complex
etiology of the sickness.

The incantation scene on the Assyrian bronze tablet
(illustration p. 29), used as an amulet, shows us the spiritual
situation of the sick person better than any description. The
bearded sick person is lying on his bed (middle strip), his hand
raised in prayer, no doubt to the gods whose symbols are
reproduced in the upper row. From the left, horn caps (Anu),
ram's head on a stake (Ea), bundle of lightning (Adad), grave staff
(Marduk), writing utensil (Nabu), eight-pointed star (Ishtar),
winged sun (Shamash), moon crescent (Shin), and seven stars.
These represent the upper world, heaven, light. To the right and
left of the sickbed stand two incantation priests dressed as fish
(ašipu) with vessels for purification water from which they
sprinkle the sick person with small plant bundles (?) ("purge me
with hyssop . . . ," Ps. 51:7 can be compared here). The frame
with the lamp on it at the right also appears to belong to this
ceremony, which appears to be in full progress. What is actually
taking place here is graphically-symbolically portrayed in the
scenes around the incantation scene. The threatening fever
demon, probably Labartu or Lamashtu, with a lion's head,
double-headed snakes in each hand, demonic animals (swine,

dog) at each breast—this fever demon is itself threatened by another winged demon with a raised arm (at the far left)—the same figure we find on the reverse side of the tablet, also peering over the upper edge; they withdraw into the swamp or reed area where they are at home, kneeling on a horse or ass (?), which itself is trotting in a ship. The scene to the right of the sickbed portrays the same action in a similar fashion, the sickness demons are apparently being fought, overcome, and led away by other demonlike and divine beings. This exorcism is taking place on the level of ritual (field above the sickness scene) by the appearance of the seven priests with animal masks and raised right hands. The objects on the right in the lower section are perhaps to be taken as sacrificial vessels for the sickness demons.

The cosmic aspect of this reproduction is particularly interesting—in view of Psalms 41, 51, 88, and others as well. The sick person's case takes in a wide scope on earth, in two nether and one upper world realm (one spoke earlier about a "Hades relief"). It sets things in motion that begin in the social and cultic-ritualistic realm and touch on the entire living world, including gods and demons. It precipitates struggles in the middle realm where the spirits fight over the sick person, and only the employment of the powers of the upper world through the Ea-priests is able to rescue him.

Two completely different texts appear to be characteristic for the social situation of the sick person and physician. First we have the passage in the Sumerian myth, Enki and Ninmah, speaking about the creation of the sick and crippled. In the intoxication of a festival—the narrative tells us—both gods had a wager. Ninmah made human figures out of clay, and Enki was to determine their fate and create bread and life-supporting material for them. She created six figures, among them a sterile woman and a eunuch, and immediately their place in the social order was determined by Enki: in the "woman's house" and in court service. Then the roles were reversed. Enki created and brought about such a cripple that Ninmah—in spite of great effort—had to confess her inability to accord such a being a place in society.[32]

This myth teaches us that the sick and crippled are victims of the whims of the gods; they can be socially integrated in part, but on the other hand, their existence appears to be so senseless and worthless that even their creators look in vain for a place to put them. A document of resignation in the face of mankind's suffering!

The other text, a farce on the false physician called "The Story of the Poor Man of Nippur," was found in Sultanepe in Asia Minor and originated in all likelihood in ancient Babylonian times. It gives us a unique look at that period's daily life.[33] Three episodes portray the jokes a poor man plays out of revenge on the mayor of the city of Nippur. The second of these episodes shows him disguised as a physician with a clean-shaven head, a loincloth, a libation vessel and an incense vessel. He tries to convince the suffering rich person by means of not particularly modest self-recommendations that he is a medicinal authority, and he treats the deceived patient with all sorts of methods. The trick succeeds, apparently because the role of the physician and his style were so securely fixed and clear-cut that the expectations a sick person associated with a physician's activities were easily satisfied. Nonetheless the image of the physician, asû, belonged in the overall city picture as early as the old Babylonian period, even though mockery and criticism by contemporaries accompanied him from an equally early period.

The medical texts of the Hittites[34] and Persians,[35] both of whom appear to be influenced by the culture of the Fertile Crescent, offer us a picture essentially no different than that we have just seen. In the Hittite language, the word physician (^{LU}A.ZU) was written as a Sumerian loan word. He was "a therapist as well as a magician," and sicknesses were accordingly treated both medicinally and magically, thus reflecting the general oriental understanding of sickness. The "priest-physicians and medical arts of old Persia" also appear to fit into this overall framework, though direct influences on ancient Israel in this context have not yet been established.

7. Egypt

In antiquity, Egypt had already long been considered a center and stronghold of medical science. In Homer's *Odyssey* we read: "There everyone is a physician and surpasses all men as regards experience." (Od. IV 220-32) This reputation was based primarily on extremely early collections of medicinal experiences. The famous Ebers Papyrus, for example, a 20-meter long product of the Old Empire, "collects 877 prescriptions for 250 illnesses."[36] The Smith Papyrus, the oldest surgical textbook, "differentiates with utter strictness between the examination method, diagnosis, therapy or prescription, and prognosis."[37] The legendary physician and wise man Imhotep virtually embodied the art and power of healing. Furthermore, a number of unique pictorial representations of sick people come from Egypt, including a stele of someone suffering from infantile paralysis, a relief of the princes of Punt who were suffering from adiposity, portrayals of blind harpists, and several more. The examinations of mummies were particularly revealing for the history of sickness and disease.

A rich source of medicinal aid apparently stood at the disposal of a sick person in Egypt, though it is, of course, difficult to say to what extent any individual actually had access to it.[38] Perhaps the more spectacular medicinal successes overshadowed general health conditions, but nonetheless, one does get the impression that at certain times things were in better shape in Egypt than elsewhere. If treatment by a physician was actually employed, things proceeded in an extremely orderly manner, with a diagnosis, therapy, and prognosis. The physician decided whether it was an illness he would treat (1), an illness with which he would have to struggle (2), or an illness one could not treat at all (3).[39] Above all, in the last case, the Egyptian, too, would seek refuge in a magical procedure which itself was no doubt often overseen by the knowledgeable physician. The example of the Edwin Smith Papyrus is informative in this context. On the front side of this "wound book" from the Old Empire we find forty-eight surgical cases described and treated in a sophisticated, scientific fashion. On the reverse side of the same papyrus, however, we find all sorts of incantations and magical sayings against pestilence. This is a picture similar to the one from the Fertile Crescent: "To be sure, at a very early date medicine had moved by means of observation, experience, experiment, and combination from the magical beliefs of prehistory to a neat and tidy science; but that magic continued to accompany it like a shadow, and during the period of cultural decline at the end of Egyptian history it overran medicine once again. In the later period one's confidence was centered more and more on amulets . . . and magical steles . . . and incantation formulas."[40]

In Egypt, too, one finds the same distribution of roles as in the Fertile Crescent. In both places we have the practical physician who works with healing substances, feels the pulse, makes incisions, and so on. The incantation priest *(āsipu)* there, is represented by the so-called "lectionary priest" here, actually the "bearer of the festive role" or exorcist who "casts a spell on the sick visage and conjures the (foul) smell"—as he characterizes himself.[41]

In addition to the documents from the Theban grave city still to be discussed, several private documents of sick persons are both moving and graphic; an example is the letter of a blind man to his son:

"Do not turn away from me. It does not do well with me at all. Do not cease to weep for me, for I am in darkness. My Lord Amun has departed from me. But do please bring me a bit of honey for my eyes and also fat from . . . and genuine lead glance. Do it, do it really. Am I then not your father? I am just so miserable because whenever I want to use my eyes, they are not there."[42]

8. Influences During the Later Period

It seems as if the Israel of the Old Testament only came into contact with medicine during the Hellenistic period. The Greek medicine associated with the name Hippocrates, just as was the case with Egyptian medicine, initially had no recognizable effect on the daily life of Palestinian Israel as "a science and craft."[43] The following example from Plato's *Republic* is hardly thinkable within the Jewish sphere before Sirach 38 (about 190), even though one finds a more frequent mentioning of "physicians" in the later writings: "When a carpenter is sick, he expects his physician to give him medicine which will act as emetic for the sickness, or he expects to be rid of the illness by means of purging or burning out or by means of the knife" (III 15, 406 D).

On the other hand, one notices the increasing colorfulness of the exorcism rites which find a place in Israel's Old Testament writings and are rejected less vehemently and sharply. The oriental influence could no longer be stemmed and controlled during the Exile (at the very latest).[44] The legend of Tobit (around 200 B.C.) allows the pious Israelite to use medicinal and magical healing methods, and even traces them back to a recommendation of an angel of God. Indeed, Tobit's blindness is healed in precisely this manner (see B. I).

According to the Old Testament documents, the situation of the sick person in Israel differentiated itself from that in cultures surrounding Israel in four points, which in conclusion we can summarize as follows:

(1) In general a sick person had virtually no *aids* at his disposal worth mentioning, no physicians in the real sense, and no knowledge of medicine.

(2) In general he had access to *no* really recognized or tolerated healing procedures or *practices*, including no ritualistic incantations or exorcism-related manipulations.

(3) Well into the later period, a sick person in ancient Israel was limited in both directions, and these limitations reduced his possibilities both in general and in principle. That sick person in ancient Israel did not have immediate access to that which was so readily available to the blind father from Amarna, the mayor of Nippur, the carpenter from Syracuse, or the unknown person with the amulet from Chadattu. Here he met with limitations and hindrances.

(4) The sick person in Israel had undisturbed, unconditional access to only one path—at least according to the Old Testament—if he wanted to comprehend his illness religiously; namely to turn to his God in supplication and prayer.

II. Statements Concerning Sickness in the Old Testament Literature: Available Texts

Because of the broad dissemination of material, it is best to look first for an ordering principle. The chronological-historical sequence is ill-suited for this, because in the case of most documents, a chronological determination is not at all, or only barely, possible (for instance, in the psalms). An artificial chronological framework would also suggest that a continuous line is discernible between the texts and textual passages. This can succeed only in a preliminary fashion and will be attempted in a synthetic section at the end (chap. IV). The systematic-theological schema also appears ill-suited for adequately comprehending the profusion of disparate material; such a schema would be an attempt to order the statements according to their dogmatic content (for example: sickness as punishment, as a test, as education, and so on). But this system presupposes that the Old Testament statements about sickness comprise a unity transcending the texts themselves, be it in the sense of a historical development or a successive accumulation—something that first would have to be proven. It seems best here to choose a third path, the literary-historical one. One collects what is said about sickness or sick people in the various basic forms of speech or broader literary categories, and thus acquires an internal historical, as well as a systematic, ordering principle and also direct access to the variously portrayed situations.

1. Narrative Literature

In many passages the Old Testament speaks more or less at length about sicknesses and sick people, since sickness and healing are an event, a process, or a "story" which is most easily comprehended by one's narrating it. A narrative tries to understand and recount something, tries to communicate and thus "repeats" what has happened, and tries to translate and interpret. It presupposes both distance and nearness, comprehends the unusual within the usual, creates a past world with its values anew from within and places it into the context of those it addresses. Particularly in its biblical form, it is a splendid way to portray realities such as sickness in an encompassing manner. "By the way," writes K. H. Miskotte when citing F. Rosenzweig, "a teaching or doctrine already inheres within the secret of form of the biblical narrative itself, in the sequence of events, in the accents and turns, above all in a dialogical element which tenses the narrative into a framework of question and answer, diction and contradiction, sentence and clause."[45] We are concerned here with that "teaching or doctrine."

The motif of the matriarch's infertility plays an important role in the older narratives of Genesis, whose roots reach back to the patriarchal family clans. This stands in sharp contrast to the motif of the promise of sons and heirs, for example, in Genesis 15. One might, of course, inquire whether childlessness in the sense of the patriarchal narratives is to be considered a sickness (ḥŏlî). One should probably give the question an affirmative answer. In the (Yahwistic) version of the narrative about the threatening of the matriarch in Genesis 12, the Pharaoh is punished by Yahweh with "great plagues" for having taken Sarah, Abraham's wife, as his own wife (12:17). According to the other (Elohist) version (Gen. 20), the punishment is childlessness. In a concluding sentence there we also read something about the cause of childlessness: "For the Lord had closed all the wombs of the house of Abimelech" (20:18). The directness of the effect and the dependence of man's physical life on Yahweh could not be more drastically expressed. Genesis 21:1 speaks then in a similar manner about Yahweh's "seeking" Sarah and "doing" something to her so she could bear a son.

The narrative of Jacob's struggle at Jabbok tells a similar story (Gen. 32:23 ff). The "touch of the hollow of his thigh," resulting in Jacob's limp, is based, at least in the later stages of transmission, on the same idea of a direct intercession by the deity. On the other hand, the patriarchal narratives speak more incidentally—without particular emphasis on interpretation and without religious implication—about the blindness that comes with age (Gen. 27:1; 48:1, 10 and later also), and about the pain of wounds, for example during circumcision (Gen. 34:25). One could speak of these things in both ways according to the particular narrator's point of view and inclination.

Compared to the patriarchal narratives with their concentration on familiar problems, the horizon of several other Pentateuch narratives appears to be more extensive: Exodus 15; Numbers 12; 21; 25. Whereas in the former it was infertility, the weakness of old age, and the pain of wounds, here it is a matter (as in Gen. 12) of plagues and epidemics, and of ṣara at, leprosy, thus of sickness of a collective nature or of collective significance. The social framework of these narratives is probably the larger community of trans-family units, grouped around the "assembly tent" and delimited by the "camp." We find in them, perhaps, reflections of the nomadic period and desert wanderings. Plagues and pestilence were considered Yahweh's collective punishment; snakes bite at his command (Num. 21:6), and the pestilence is sent by him (Num. 14:12; 25:8 f). Miriam's "leprosy" is, according to Numbers 12 (primary layer), punishment for her opposition to Moses' leadership claim: "And the anger of the Lord was kindled against them, and he departed; and when the cloud removed from over the tent, behold, Miriam was leprous, as white as snow" (Num. 12:9).

This narrative is instructive in many respects. It offers some extremely old views and customs concerning "leprosy." The leper is compared to a miscarriage whose flesh is already half-decomposed, i.e., he is already considered a corpse. But this "leprosy" can be healed, and the healing is followed by a purification. "If her father had but spit in her face, should she not be shamed seven days? Let her be shut up outside the camp seven days, and after that she may be brought in again." The narrative reflects a structural theological implication whose origin can be ascertained only with difficulty, though it also inheres in the story of the threatening of the matriarch (Gen. 20) and the story of the bronze serpent (Num. 21). We are speaking of the healing by Yahweh on the basis of a confession of guilt and intercession. "And Aaron said to Moses, 'Oh, my Lord, do not punish us because we have done foolishly and have sinned.' . . . And Moses cried to the Lord, 'Heal her, O God, I beseech thee.' " Moses is to make a bronze serpent against snake-bite and erect it on a stake as a curative symbol.[46]

Both healing cases reflect procedures that, in the first case, consist of a sacral-cultic penitential rite, in the second a magical practice. The implications of the illness event become clear— social, cultic, or magical—but also its integration into the overall course of events between Yahweh and his people.

The narratives from the emerging time of the kings have their own unique character, and the horizon is broadened under the influence of the royal court. The narrator of the ark story (1 Sam. 6) and of the story of David's rise (1 Sam. 19) is interested in foreign and archaic forms of religion. The narrative of Nabal betrays as physiological interest (1 Sam. 25): "And in the morning, when the wine had gone out of Nabal, his wife told him these things, and his heart died within him, and he became as a stone. And about ten days later the Lord smote Nabal; and he died" (25:37 f). Psychological reactions become visible[47] (concerning Saul, see III, 2). Seers and prophets play a role, and court wisdom illuminates the sickness' manifestation. Two narrative structures can serve as examples. 1 Samuel 6 speaks with a humorous attractiveness about the Philistines' helplessness in the face of the tumor plague. Nonetheless, their priests and soothsayers recognize the true cause and true culprit and advise them to send the ark back along with retribution, "then you will be healed." They are to offer "five golden tumors (?) and five golden mice" as magic images; then they will recognize by certain signs (something that, even in Israel, was not always completely clear?) whether the "God of Israel" has brought this upon them. If "it is not his hand that struck us," then—this is a thoroughly modern alternative—"it happened to us by chance" (compare v 9). The listeners and readers should know better!

The tone of 2 Samuel 12 is more serious and weighty. The child of David and Bathsheba was sick, for "Yahweh had struck it" (compare v 1). David, as the person concerned, assumes the posture of the penitent, seeks Yahweh, fasts, grieves, and sleeps upon the ground. That was no doubt customary in such cases. The child dies. David reacts to the news in a completely unexpected manner. He washes, anoints himself, changes his clothes, prays in the house of the Lord, and ceases to fast. Asked about his odd behavior, he answers bitterly: "But now he is dead; why should I fast? Can I bring him back again? I shall go to him, but he will not return to me" (v 23).

The narrator interprets David's reaction differently. According to Nathan's words, the child died for David's own guilt. Its death renders the forgiveness effective. These events are quite complicated, but the narrators have acquired a deep insight into the circumstances in which a sickness can become a comprehensible sign through which God speaks, just as he did through the sign of Moses' "leprous hand" (Exod. 4:6).

Prophets, as proclaimers and representatives of Yahweh, are confronted with cases of sickness in a series of narratives from the time of the kings. They are asked for advice, primarily by kings, and thus function as the givers of oracles who know the answers to the question of whether the concerned person will recover from a sickness. These prophetic, or better, "Word of Yahweh," legends—have individual characteristics. In 2 Samuel 24 Gad threatens with Yahweh's punishment, but leaves the choice to David. He chooses pestilence as royal punishment in order to give himself over into the hand of Yahweh. In 2 Samuel 12 Nathan announces forgiveness for David; nonetheless, the child's sickness and death remain as a (surrogate) punishment. The blind Ahija of Silo, in 1 Kings 14, has only "heavy tidings" for the king who is cast aside by Yahweh. By means of prayer and magic, Elijah is able to bring about the healing by Yahweh of a child who was punished for the sins of the mother (1 Kings 17:17 ff); Elisha is able to do similar things (2 Kings 4:15 ff). Behind closed doors he prays, lays himself upon the child, putting his mouth upon its mouth, his eyes upon its eyes, and his hands upon its hands, stretches himself upon the child, warms it, gets up, goes up again, stretches himself upon it again until the child sneezes seven times and opens its eyes. The "leprous" officer (2 Kings 5), however, is disappointed that Elisha tells him to bathe seven times in the Jordan. He had thought "that he would surely come out to me, and stand, and call on the name of the Lord his God, and wave his hand over the place, and cure the leper" (vv 11 f).[48]

In 2 Kings 8:7 ff, Elisha's falsified oracle concerning the sickness of the Syrian king precipitates the regicide. The Isaiah of the legends, finally, comes first as a bearer of bad tidings to the sick Hezekiah, then the second time as the bringer of Yahweh's forgiveness to the king's penitential prayer. In addition, he also knows the cure—a cake of figs—and can offer a sign (2 Kings 20; Isa. 38 f).

Elijah's question in 2 Kings 1 to the messengers of the unfortunate king Ahaziah is exemplary for the common concern of all these legends: "Is it because there is no God in Israel that you are going to inquire of Baalzebub, the god of Ekron?" (1:3). Sickness, even the sickness of a king, indeed even of a non-Israelite king or officer, is the concern of Yahweh, the God of Israel. To him alone can one turn with any chance of success; he alone can determine the outcome, for he alone decrees sickness as punisment for guilt. That is why sickness becomes a theme of the prophets, since it is a matter of interaction, and emerges from one's relationship to God. This is also why there is healing as forgiveness, as a miracle, since Yahweh alone is a God who can kill and make alive—as the definition reads in 2 Kings 5:7. Thus there is even the return on the path without return (2 Sam. 12:23). As an interpersonal matter between God and man, sickness demands a corresponding behavior, penitential like David's or supplicating like Hezekiah's. Both magical and medicinal elements can acquire a legitimate function here, integrated into the prayer and sanctioned by the prophet. Healing, however, is accomplished just as was the sickness itself: as an effect on the level of Yahweh's word.

The narratives belonging exclusively to the Chronicler are characterized by a stronger interest in the manifestations and consequences of sickness, no doubt corresponding to a higher level of medicinal knowledge. In 2 Chronicles 16:11 ff we hear that King Asa was struck by a serious foot ailment, but that he—the orthodox narrator chides the enlightened king!—turned in his sickness to the physicians instead of to Yahweh, something which apparently did not help him: he died two years later. In a legendary letter in 2 Chronicles 21:12 ff, the prophet Elija announces to King Jehoram an affliction by "a severe sickness"; and indeed, "the Lord smote him in his bowels with an incurable disease" so that in the course of time "his bowels came out because of the disease, and he died in great agony." Finally, in the legend of King Uzziah in 2 Chronicles 26:16, "leprosy" breaks out on his forehead when he illicitly brings incense into the temple. We hear about that "separate house" in which the king lived until his death "because he was excluded from the temple." Sickness is still unambiguously the affair of Yahweh. He smites, and he is responsible for the healing. Nonetheless, the tone of these narratives tells us that people are now attempting—even the Chronicler, in spite of his chiding—to turn their attention to the objectively given situations, to describe them and explain them.

Three Wisdom narratives[49] and edifying legends still remain that throw a unique light on the situation concerning sickness: the Job narrative (1–2; 42), the narrative about Tobit (1–14), and the legendary edict of Nebuchadnezzar (Dan. 3:31–4:34). All three encompass Wisdom elements, sketch in a model, and expound a doctrine.

The prose narrative about the pious Job[50] teaches model behavior for a situation of misfortune, behavior proving itself by acceptance and surrender: "The Lord gave, and the Lord has taken away; blessed be the name of the Lord" (1:21). And even when struck by the most horrible sickness, in the form of loathsome sores: "Shall we receive good at the hand of God, and shall we not receive evil?" (2:10). This kind of standing true clears the way for the decisive turn: "And the Lord restored the fortunes of Job . . . and the Lord gave Job twice as much as he had before" (42:10). Full rehabilitation also means recognition by one's fellow men. They do not come after the successful healing in order to express their sympathy, but rather celebrate a common meal with him, console him, and each give him a piece of money (Hebrew *qesitah*) and a gold ring—all as a sign of the healed person's social restitution.

The legend of Tobit pursues, among others, the goal of showing its readers the finely spun thread guiding human life, even when misfortunes such as total blindness occur. God then sends help in the form of angels who teach men how to come to terms with the misfortune. This includes mysterious medicines such as the liver, heart, and gall of a fish[51] as well as magical curative rites to exorcize demons. The legend, a product of the Eastern Diaspora, legitimizes such means by saying the angel Raphael himself mediated them; this opens the door to exorcism and folk-medicinal practices, a door from Persia which had hitherto been officially closed—as the demon name Asmodeus suggests.

The fictional edict of Nebuchadnezzar in the book of Daniel is, a far as its literary character is concerned, a so-called exhomologesis,[52] a public praise-confession to the God who struck him with madness and then healed him again; in various guises it can be expected of every person involved in such cases of illness.

2. Psalms

The situation of the sick person from the inner perspective of an individual's own experience is expressed in the Old Testament's literature of prayer. Since H. Gunkel, one arranges the larger part of the individual psalms—the psalms whose I-subject is an individual person—into two groups, the so-called lament psalms on the one hand, and the psalms of thanksgiving on the other. The situation will determine the point of orientation in each case, the *Sitz im Leben* out of which the group-type, or genre, emerges. For Gunkel, the paradigm was the ill supplicant who lamentingly turned to his God in the time of need and then, after successful recovery, thankfully offered up the sacrifice of praise. And indeed, both these aspects of life—lament in the form of penitential sadness, and thanksgiving in the form of an atoning praise celebration—are the concrete as well as the ideal points of departure for a large part of the psalms.

As has been shown, the psalms do speak about sickness and healing and not just about suffering of a general nature. A definite sequence of events lies behind this concern. Long-practiced customs, not only in the behavior of the person concerned, but also in the liturgical-cultic needs and variations in ritual, no doubt consolidated and expanded this sequence into, as it were, a traversable path. This path, which can also be found in other contemporary forms of religion and cult, is in part explicitly described in two Old Testament passages, Psalm 107:17-22 and Job 33:19-30, two texts that are certainly not very early ones, but rather probably from the postexilic period.

According to these texts, the psalm of the individual sick person was variously anchored in the lament phase and was a prayer for preservation and healing. In keeping with this context, it was often simultaneously a confession of guilt and a request for mercy, spoken within the private sickroom, probably with the aid of a priest. It was very likely not performed by the sick person himself during a pilgrimage to a holy place, since anyone seriously sick was generally not up to the rigors of such a trip. Or the psalm belonged in the thanksgiving phase as a laudatory prayer and personal (sacrificial) contribution within the frame-work of a community meal, celebrated at the sanctuary after successful recovery and as part of the reconciliation and rehabilitation of the recovered person. This could happen to a man "twice, three times" during the course of life. The actual, individual, and liturgically formed psalms of sickness originated in this way.

Let us follow this path by looking at a few examples. "But I, when they were sick—I wore sackcloth, I afflicted myself with fasting. I prayed with head bowed on my bosom, as though I grieved for my friend or my brother; I went about as one who laments his mother, bowed down and in mourning" (Ps. 35:13 f). The psalmist speaks about the solidarity of his sympathy with the sick by performing mourning rites with and for them and by offering prayers.

Psalm 38, for example, appears to be such a prayer; its words still enable us to recognize the context of penitential rites:

> O Lord, rebuke me not in thy anger
> nor chasten me in thy wrath!
> For thy arrows have sunk into me,
> and thy hand has come down on me.
> There is no soundness in my flesh
> because of thy indignation;
> there is no health in my bones
> because of my sin.
> For my iniquities have gone over my head;
> they weigh like a burden too heavy for me.
> My wounds grow foul and fester
> because of my foolishness,
> I am utterly bowed down and prostrate;
> all the day I go about mourning.

The data are not sufficient to identify this supplicant's illness, although he occasionally offers an extremely precise description; for example, the graphic portrayal of his pounding pulse ("my heart throbs," *seharhar*). A medicinal diagnosis means nothing to him because he views his own case in a different context, a context he interprets in part conceptually as a punishment for guilt that Yahweh has brought upon him in anger because of his "foolishness." He also interprets it in part in a graphic, metaphorical fashion in the statement about "Yahweh's hand" and "Yahweh's arrows" that have struck him. Thus he reacts as prescribed, assumes the role of the penitent, goes around in sackcloth and ashes, observes the period of silence, wakes, fasts, offers his lament to Yahweh, confesses his guilt and pleads for mercy from him who is causing this.

The same holds true for the supplicant in Psalm 39, except that his situation is made even more desperate because of additional, self-incurred aggravation (a curse). The supplicant in Psalm 88 identifies his own situation as that of someone who is already dead, indeed of a dead person of inferior status: a "forsaken" one, who like "those whom thou dost remember no more" could expect only a desolate, shadowy existence in the underworld. The supplicants in Psalm 69 (as well as 22) speak similarly in the first part, as do those in Psalms 6 and 102.

Most of these lament prayers and penitential texts open up

yet another dimension to us, which at first glance appears totally incomprehensible. The environment has a hostile effect on the sick person. This phenomenon is peculiarly strange, but if one refers back to the social relationships found, for example, in Job 19, things become clearer. We have to remember this was a society that considered the sick person to be stigmatized, or at least marked by guilt, and in which no remedies were known for many or almost all sicknesses; the sick person was thus thrown back upon the care and sustenance of his environment or surroundings, an environment with hardly enough for itself. Precious little space remained in such a society for this kind of case. To this one can add speculators, personal enemies, fanatics. . . .

We find an impressive image of this in the suffering person's penitential prayer included as a citation in Psalm 41:4-10, a convalescent's thanksgiving psalm of praise:

> As for me, I said, "O Lord, be gracious to me;
> heal me, for I have sinned against thee!"
> My enemies say of me in malice:
> "When will he die, and his name perish?"!
> And when one comes to see me, he utters
>   empty words,
> while his heart gathers mischief;
> when he goes out, he tells it abroad.
> All who hate me whisper together about me;
> they imagine the worst for me.
> They say, "A deadly thing has fastened upon
>   him;
> he will not rise again from where he lies."
> Even my bosom friend in whom I trusted,
> who ate of my bread, has lifted his heel
>   against me.
> But do thou, O Lord, be gracious to me,
> And raise me up, that I may requite them!

Three hostile parties can be recognized: the false friend, the hypocritical visitor and acquaintance, and the group of enemies "abroad" whose talk and plans the sick person hears. They all speculate about his demise; their words sound brutal, false, and cynical. Apparently this hurts the psalmist more (in retrospect) than his illness, of which he speaks at the beginning and which he was totally prepared to accept as justified. As far as he is concerned, however, this kind of treatment goes beyond any standard imposed by God's own punishment.

Healing is also considered by the psalmist to be a direct intervention by God in one's life. The process can be called or described as a miracle (verb *rp'*), to be sure, but in actuality it lies so far outside his own realm of accessible experience that he can hardly reach any real understanding of it. To this extent it then becomes a model for divine intervention in general. The accessible part of the healing process, then, is the religious and social implications and consequences, and here institutional aids stood ready to rehabilitate the convalescent cultically, and thus to reintegrate him socially. The recovered person would generally set out to regain his integrity at the holy place and let it be publicly affirmed, an integrity that, within the guilt-punishment system of thought, had apparently been endangered or lost.

> Then man prays to God, and he accepts him,
> he comes into his presence with joy.
> He recounts (returns) to men his salvation.
> (Job 33:26)

"Salvation" *(ṣedaqa)* means "communal salvation" as a cultically mediated gift enabling the recipient to do justice to the social relationships in which he stands. He is reintegrated in every sense, and this event places him at the beginning of a new life; possible communal violations within the framework described above can now be put aside or mediated, or perhps even legally prosecuted. The thanksgiving or hymnic psalms—which themselves have this kind of legal function—speak about this from various perspectives.

> And he sings before men, and says:
> "I sinned, and perverted what was right,

and it was not requited to me.
He has redeemed my soul from going down into
  the Pit,
and my life shall see the light." (Job 33:27 f)

Both Psalms 32 and 103, as well as other indications inside and
outside the Psalter, suggest that penitence or the forgiveness of
sins was a part of the rites of restitution, and had its center in a
pronouncement of acquittal. The exact sequence can only be
partially reconstructed, though it may be reflected in the
beginning of Psalm 103.

Bless the Lord, O my soul;
and all that is within me,
bless his holy name!
Bless the Lord, O my soul,
and forget not all his benefits,
who forgives all your iniquity,
who heals all your diseases,
who redeems your life from the Pit,
who crowns you with steadfast love and mercy,
who satisfies you with good as long as you live
so that your youth is renewed like the eagle's. (vv 1-5)

The supplicant in Psalm 41 is able to utilize the penitential
sequence, as a result of the healing process, against his enemies.
"By this I know that thou art pleased with me, in that my enemy
has not triumphed over me. But thou hast upheld me because of
my integrity, and set me in thy presence for ever" (41:12 ff).
Joyous hope emerges from the cultic reconciliation which
confirms the *tom*, the element of salvation and health. This had to
be overcome in the meantime because he had confessed guilt in a
penitential prayer.
     The psalm's final verse speaks about how Yahweh has
erected an eternal monument in his own "presence" by means of
the healing itself manifested in the person of the supplicant. This
motif alludes to the fact that the recovered person felt obligated
to immortalize his praise and penitential thanksgiving in the form

of a public confession above and beyond the actual psalm recitation (before the community). Both Psalms 41 and 30, as well as an apocryphal fragment of an alphabetical poem from Qumran, confirm this by proving to be votive gifts themselves, in written form, dedicated to the holy place. Isaiah 38, the Hezekiah psalm, is redactionally called a royal thanksgiving psalm and is described as a "writing." Examples of such steles are also known to us from the Egyptian Amarna.[53] As far as form and content are concerned, they stand closest to Psalm 30. In both instances, sickness and healing become a matter of public and cultic interest, both touching and changing the social environment beyond the life of the person involved.

The following text is exemplary and in places extremely illuminating, not only as regards the inner situation of the sick person in Oriental antiquity, but also concerning how personal piety expresses itself in this situation. The text belongs to the genre of Sumerian cultic poetry characterized as a "letter to God" or "letter-prayer." These are prayers in letter form written down so that they can be recited and offered up at the cultic center, since the author himself is not able to appear there. They are closely parallel to, and possibly even the forerunners and models of, the Old Testament lament psalms. In many characteristics and motifs the text resembles the prayer psalms (for example, Pss. 22; 30; 41), but goes beyond them to the extent that it offers us important details concerning the composition and origin of such texts, details which, in the Psalter, have to a large extent fallen victim to stylization and leveling. Not least for this reason—illuminating anew what has already been said—let us reproduce the entire text here.[54]

The author, Sin-šamuh, who is ill, writes to his god Enki.

To Enki, the outstanding Lord of heaven and earth,
    whose nature is unequaled
Speak!
To Nudimmud, the prince of broad understanding
who determines fates together with An,
Who distributes the appropriate divine attributes
    among the Anunnaki, whose course cannot be [reversed]

i

The omniscient one who is given intelligence
    from sunrise to sunset,
    the lord of knowledge, the king of sweet waters,
    the god who begot me,
Say furthermore!

ii

(This is) what Sin-šamuh, the scribe,
    the son of Ur-Nin [. . .], your servant, says:
Since the day that you created me,
    you have [given] me an education.
I have not been negligent toward the name,
    by which you are called, like a father [. . .].
I did not plunder your offerings at the festivals
    to which I go regularly.

iii

[But] now, whatever I do, the judgment
    of my sin is not [. . .]
My fate has come my way, I am lifted
    onto a place of destruction, I cannot find a omen.
A hostile deity has verily brought sin my way,
    I cannot find (?) its side.
On the day that my vigorous house was
    decreed by Heaven
There is no keeping silent about my sin,
    I must answer for it.

iv

I lie down on a bed of alas and alack,
    I intone the lament.
My goodly figure is bowed down to the ground,
    I am sitting on (my) feet.
My [. . .] is lifted from (its) place, my features
    are changed.
[. . .] restlessness is put into my feet,
    my life ebbs away.
The bright day is made like an "alloyed" day
    for me, I slip into my grave.

v

I am a scribe, (but) whatever I have been taught
    has been turned into spittle(?) for me
My hand is "gone" for writing, my mouth
    is inadequate for dialogue.
I am not old, (yet) my hearing is heavy,
    my glance cross-eyed.
Like a brewer (?) with a junior term(?) I am
    deprived of the right to seal.
Like a wagon of the highway whose yoke has been
    broken(?) I am placed on the road

vi

Like an apprentice-diviner who has left his
    master's house I am slandered ignobly.
My acquaintance does not approach me,
    speaks never a word with me,
My friend will not take counsel with me,
    will not put my mind at rest.
The taunter has made me enter the tethering-rope,
    my fate has made me strange.
Oh my god, I rely on you,
    what have I to do with man?!

vii

I am grown-up, how am I to spread out in a narrow place?
My house (is) a plaited nest, I am not satisfied
    with its attractiveness.
My built-up houses are not faced with brick(?)
Like little (female) cedars, planted in a dirty place,
    I(?) bear no fruit.
Like a young date palm planted by the
    side of a boat, I produce no foliage.

viii

I am (still) young, must I walk about thus
    before my time? Must I roll around in the dust?
In a place where my mother and father
    are not present I am detained,
    who will recite my prayer to you?

In a place where my kinsmen do not gather
I am overwhelmed, who will bring my offering in to you?

ix

Damgalnunna, your beloved first wife,
May she bring to you like my mother, may she
introduce my lament before you.
Asalalimnunna, son of the abyss,
May he bring it to you like my father,
may he introduce my lament before you.
May he recite my lamentation to you,
may he introduce my lament before you.

x

When I have verily brought (my) sin
to you, cleanse (?) me from evil!
When you have looked upon me in the place
where I am cast down, approach my chamber!
When you have turned my dark place into daylight,
I will surely dwell in your gate of Guilt-Absolved,
I will surely sing your praises!
I will surely tear up my sin like a thread,
I will surely proclaim your exaltation!

xi

As you reach the place of heavy sin,
I will surely [sing your] praises.
Release me at the mouth of the grave,
[save me] at the head of my tomb!
(Then) I will surely appear to the people,
all the nation will verily know!
Oh my god, I am the one who reveres you!
Have mercy on the letter which I have
deposited before you!

xii

May the heart of my god be restored!

The richness of information and insights expressed by the
supplicants in the psalms is only alluded to by this sketch,[55] and

the cultic structural framework can only offer a point of orientation within the seas of thoughts and ideas. Each psalm text, however, has its own individual cosmos, and this experiential richness proves to be inexhaustible for the systematically-anthropologically interested interpreter. We see, for example, how Psalm 102 describes the supplicant's situation with a series of comparisons from nature and the world of animals ("I lie awake, I am like a lonely bird on the housetop," 102:7). Psalm 69 shows itself straight away to be a psalm of someone accused in court ("What I did not steal must I now restore?" 69:4). Psalms 42 and 43 are the poems of someone forced to remain in a foreign country because of broken limbs (42:11?), and have Zion as their main motif, while Psalm 30 claims to be like a water container which God has drawn up from the deep well (30:1), and announces a dance in which one is "girded with gladness" (30:11). Finally we can add the statements "My God, my God, why hast thou forsaken me?" (Ps. 22) and "Nevertheless I am continually with thee" (Ps. 73), as well as much more.

This richness becomes really accessible only when the authors themselves give their experiences a cultic structure; above all, when they reflect on them in the manner of the Wisdom tradition and raise them to the level of general statements over and above the situation of the sick person. We find these conditions fulfilled, however, primarily in the previously mentioned Wisdom literature.

In conclusion, let us pick up on one final aspect from that richness of imagery, namely the death-motif stereotypically associated with the image of sickness. The sick person feels near to death, or believes himself to be caught in the flow of those who are descending to the Pit; indeed, he already feels himself leaning toward the underworld, toward Sheol, the collecting center for all the living. "His soul draws near the Pit" (Job 33:22); his soul draws near to "the gates of death" (Ps. 107:18). Particularly when considering the lack of effective countermeasures, we can see how sickness, in extreme cases, is understood to be a preliminary form of death.[56] The psalms give frequent expression to this feeling:

I said, In the noontide of my days I must depart;
I am consigned to the gates of Sheol
for the rest of my years.
I said, I shall not see the Lord
in the land of the living;
I shall look upon man no more
among the inhabitants of the world.
My dwelling is plucked up and
removed from me
like a shepherd's tent;
like a weaver I have rolled up my life;
he cuts me off from the loom.
(Psalm of Hezekiah, Isa. 38:10 ff)

I sink in deep mire,
where there is no foothold;
I have come into deep waters,
and the flood sweeps over me (Ps. 69:2)

However—and this makes these texts so significant—the lament
does not just linger with statements concerning physical pain and
suffering. On the contrary, in the condition of sickness it laments
being forsaken by God, and laments God's absence, which is
being expressed. This is why God's intervention is repeatedly
explained by the fact that in the underworld—according to
general opinion—a relationship to God is no longer possible;
thus God cannot really consider it in his own best interest to lose
a supplicant and worshiper.

For Sheol cannot thank thee,
death cannot praise thee;
those who go down to the pit cannot hope
for thy faithfulness.
The living, the living, he thanks thee,
as I do this day. (Psalm of Hezekiah, Isa. 38:18 f)

What profit is there in my death,
if I go down to the Pit?
Will the dust praise thee?
Will it tell of thy faithfulness? (Ps. 30:9)

> For in death there is no
> remembrance of thee;
> in Sheol who can give thee praise? (Ps. 6:5)

Thus the miracle of healing can also be understood as a rescue from death and the underworld.

> I will extol thee, O Lord, for
> thou hast drawn me up . . .
> O Lord, thou hast brought up my
> soul from Sheol,
> restored me to life from among
> those gone down to the Pit. (Ps. 30:1, 3)

Most of the time the whole weight of the experience stands behind statements such as this, and—although freed from the pain—the psalmist includes a glance at the past into his thanksgiving, indeed he often cites his earlier prayer of supplication and lament in order to show what once was and what now is.

The various stages of prayer are once more expressed in the apocryphal psalm fragment already long familiar in Syrian, and now also in Hebrew, in the psalter of Qumran, discovered in cave 11 and called 11 A Ps* 155 (Syrian Ps. Nr. 3).[57] We will use a translation from the Hebrew text fragment.[58] This is perhaps the psalm of someone sick with leprosy.

First the prayer of supplication from the time of need is cited:

> Yahweh, I called to you: Hear me!
> I stretched my hands to your holy dwelling
>   place:
> incline your ear and grant me my wish
> and do not strike down my petition!
> Build my life up and do not topple it!
> Do not give it up before the eyes of the evildoers!
> Turn the deeds of the evil from me, he the true judge.
> Yahweh, do not judge me according to my
>   transgression,
> for no living person is justified before you!

Give me insight, Yahweh, into your
  instruction
and explain your lawful decisions to me,
and many will hear your deeds,
and the crowd praises your glory!
Think of me and do not forget me
and lead me not into too great difficulties!
The transgressions of my youth remove from me,
and may my errors no longer be remembered!
Cleanse me, Yahweh, from evil plague
and do not let it back to me any longer!
Let its roots wither in me
and its leaves shall no longer grow in me!

Then, following immediately upon this, we hear the healed
person's praise of thanksgiving:

Yours is the glory, Yahweh,
therefore my plea is filled from your countenance!
To whom should I cry, that he give me,
and men—what can I yet do about (their) power?
From you, Yahweh, is my confidence:
I called: Yahweh, and he answered me.
(He healed) my broken heart.
I slumbered and slept, dreamed (recovered?),
also (I awoke).
(You supported me, Yahweh, when my heart was struck:
and I named) Yahweh (my savior.
Now I will experience their shame.
I have trusted in you and will not be shamed . . .
Save Israel, your faithful, Yahweh,
and the house of Jacob, your elect.)!

Even in the late Israelite period the tradition of the psalm prayer
was preserved in its entire height and depth.

3. Wisdom Literature[59]

The older proverbial sayings only touch sporadically on the
topic of sickness. This was considered to be so much the domain

of religion and magic that Wisdom would not dare approach it. Nonetheless we find several examples with a remarkable insight into elements touching on the anthropological problem.

A man's spirit will endure sickness;
but a broken spirit who can bear? (Prov. 18:14)

An experience is formulated as thesis: Man can overcome his sickness in a spiritual fashion. But the question remains: What if man's spirit is itself drawn into the suffering (by means of sickness). Other proverbs also mention this body-spirit tandem.

Hope deferred makes the heart sick,
but a desire fulfilled is a tree of life. (Prov. 13:12)

or:

A cheerful heart is a good medicine,
but a downcast spirit dries up the bones. (Prov. 17:22)

which is a kind of reversal of the question formulated above (18:14).

Finally, the psychological study of the intoxicated person in Proverbs 23:29-35 is noteworthy, as well as several aspects of the intoxicated condition.

Your eyes will see strange things,
and your mind utter perverse things.
You will be like one who lies down
in the midst of the sea,
like one who lies on the top of a mast.

These are only a few examples, but they are enough to show the beginnings of a totally different, empirical view of psycho-physical conditions and dependencies. This kind of view was apparently able to take hold even in Israel, even though it was probably limited to certain circles.

Proverbs 3:7 f sounds different. It draws the curve over to a

religious wisdom which is concerned with proper behavior
during sickness.

> Be not wise in your own eyes;
> fear the Lord, and turn away from evil.
> It will be healing to your flesh
> [health, *šr,* according to Sir. 30:15 ff]
> and refreshment to your bones.

Thus the fear of God is beneficial to health—one might see this as
a platitude if this conclusion had not been drawn against the dark
background of painful experience.

Wisdom found entrance into the cult and influenced a
particular kind of piety which found its expression in the
so-called Wisdom psalms. Two texts are particularly significant
in our context: The dogmatic penitential Psalm 32 and problem
Psalm 73. Psalm 32 teaches the meaning of penitence during
sickness and speaks from first-hand experience. It recognizes
Yahweh's disciplinary hand in suffering; he wants to lead man
(*'adam*) to a search of conscience, to a confession of guilt, and to
prayer. "I will instruct you and teach you the way you should go"
(32:8). If one neglects these steps when Yahweh's hand is resting
heavily, then things only get worse. One must seek Yahweh as
long as he can be found. "Be not like a horse or a mule, without
understanding, which must be curbed with bit and bridle, else it
will not keep with you" (32:9). Healing and forgiveness are then
possible. "Blessed is the man to whom the Lord imputes no
(more) iniquity" (32:2). The path is thus precisely described. It is
the sequential path of the penitent through the stages of
ritualistic-institutional role behavior.

Things stand differently with Psalm 73. The self-evidence of
this kind of logic—sickness as punishment or penitence, then
healing—has broken down for him because he sees how well
things go for the godless while "all day long I have been stricken,
and chastened every morning" (73:14). It is not certain he is
speaking here of sickness, but neither is it essential. The problem
of God's righteousness was solved for him when he "went into the
sanctuary of God" and came to preach in God's presence:

"Nevertheless I am continually with thee" (73:23). This proximity also guarantees a just equalization after death.

This brings us directly to the Book of Job, which struggles with the Wisdom problem of the "suffering righteous person." This problem is the theme of the prose piece as well as the dialogue and its supplements. We have already spoken briefly about the leitmotif of the narrative about the pious, sick, and rehabilitated Job. The writing itself presupposes this case and lets it be thoroughly discussed according to all the rules of Wisdom teaching. Three speech sequences follow Job's own lament (chap. 3). The three friends, Eliphaz the Temanite, Bildad the Shuhite, and Zophar the Naamathite, follow one upon the other, and Job answers each of them individually. The final speech is incomplete. God's answer (38–41) actually should have followed Job's concluding speech (29–31). The final speech sequence is now interrupted by the speeches of Elihu (32–37), which were subsequently added. Various topics are discussed, often without any recognizable order, though on the whole a dramatic movement according to the paradigm lament-answer can be recognized.[60] The speech contributions identify three positions.

(1) The friends represent the traditional Wisdom position also found, for example, in Psalm 32. Commensurate behavior in this case would be a reversal and then penitence.

> As for me, I would seek God,
> and to God would I commit my cause; . . .
> For he wounds, but he binds up;
> he smites, but his hands heal. . . .
> Behold, happy is the man whom
> God reproves;
> therefore despise not the
> chastening of the Almighty. (Job 5:8, 17 f)

Eliphaz and all the friends up to Elihu give the same advice according to the same role scheme: penitence, subjection to the chastening God!

(2) Job, however, is neither able nor willing to accept this, since he is not conscious of having willfully transgressed against God. He is not able to conclude that sickness is punishment, that one therefore must be guilty, which is the common sense of the ancient Israelite as well as the ancient Oriental interpretation of fate. Therefore he demands—in the language forms of legal complaint—an analogous legal treatment of his case.

(3) For the composer of Job, finally, there remains only the answer given in Psalm 73. God's appearance in the whirlwind—God's actual epiphany—completely overshadows any human ideas, theories, or projections in its revelation. Indeed, it lets us recognize them all as violations of God's holiness. Sickness can be a test, a reprimand, a punishment, or a pedagogical measure, but subjectively and generally one cannot say whether it is indeed one of these things in each concrete case. Universal guidelines and personal capabilities encounter an objective limit here.

Job's case will be discussed in detail later from a different perspective (III.5).

In his statements about poverty and wealth, Ecclesiastes also speaks about the phenomenon of sickness (5:12–6:5), and probably does so in a figurative sense. In line with the old tradition, he traces sickness and healing back to God's own action and understands it as that disturbance in life which comes over man just as rust comes over iron. "There is a grievous evil which I have seen . . . riches were kept by their owner to his hurt" (5:13). "This is vanity; it is a sore affliction" (6:2). The expansion of the phenomenon has been pushed to an extreme degree here and reminds us of the prophets, who also use sickness as a metaphorical predicate for other realities of human life that are difficult to comprehend.

Jesus Sirach's admonitions concerning sickness are much more practical and more oriented toward actual help; here the older proverb wisdom is carried on. These admonitions concerning moderate intake of nourishment under the heading "table habits" (31:19 ff), concerning visits to the sick as a holy obligation (7:35), and concerning the sickness of the king (10:10) all flow into the large collection of sayings concerning the theme of sickness and death (37:27–38:23). The changed spiritual situation is especially noticeable. After the admonition to eat healthily (37:30), talk turns to the physician.

> Honor the physician with the honor due him,
> according to your need of him [first justification!]—
> for [second justification!] the Lord created him;
> for healing comes from the Most High
> and he will receive a gift from the king . . .
> The Lord created medicines from the earth,
> and a sensible man will not despise them . . .
> By them he [the physician] heals and takes away
>   pain;
> the pharmacist makes of them a compound.

The suggestion "this *as well as* that", instead of the "either-or" of the Chronicler, is continued in the advice given the sick person.

> My son, when you are sick do not be negligent,
> but pray to the Lord, and he will heal you.
> Give up your faults and direct your hands aright,
> and cleanse your heart from all sin.
> Offer a sweet-smelling sacrifice
> and a memorial portion of fine flour,
> and pour oil on your offering,
> as much as you can afford.

To this extent he sounds much like a pupil of Eliphaz! And then:

> And give the physician his place,
> for the Lord created him;
> let him not leave you, for there is need of him.
> There is a time when success lies
> in the hands of physicians,
> for they too will pray to the Lord
> that he should grant them success in diagnosis
> and in healing, for the sake of preserving life.

In his conclusion he again sounds quite traditional, and offers a variation of the logical chain, but not without a mocking undertone.

He who sins before his Maker,
may he fall into the care of a physician.[61]

Wisdom reflection is here attempting to effect that synthesis
which—at that time already common practice—was to a large
extent to become the dominant *ne plus ultra* of theological
interpretations of sickness.

4. Prophecy

In the prophetic narratives already briefly discussed within
the context of the book of Kings, the prophets appeared primarily
as the recipients of oracle inquiries. Their answers were often
pronouncements that transcended the yes-no information
normally expected. Any given case was thus placed in a wider
horizon. David and Bathsheba's sick child (2 Sam. 12), the sick
children of the widow of Zarephath (1 Kings 17) and of the
Shunammite woman (2 Kings 4), or the sick king Hezekiah (2
Kings 20, par Isa. 38) all took on symbolic meaning for the
condition of the relationship to Yahweh, which was in question,
and for its climax in the confrontation with the prophetic word.
Sickness and healing proved to be acts of Yahweh which the
preclassical prophet was still authorized to influence. However,
the prophetic legends already allow us to recognize three aspects
of sickness and healing that became significant for the classical
prophets: (1) as a manner of behavior in the reaction to sickness
(self-help); (2) as a model for understanding divine action toward
groups and individuals; (3) as signs of a guilty world, thus *via
negationis* as an eschatological *topos*.

We have only a few examples of the first aspect. We hear
about an intervention during Elijah's time when the northern
Israelite king suffered an accident and sought advice from the
Philistine god of Ekron. "Is it because there is no God in Israel
that you are going to inquire of Baalzebub, the god of Ekron?" An
oracle is not solicited, but comes anyway and sounds like a
judgment. "Now therefore thus says the Lord, 'You shall not
come down from the bed to which you have gone, but you shall

surely die.' " The reason for this judgment is hidden in the question concerning the appropriateness of the venture, which the king answers contrary to the norm of faith in Israel; he thus denies Israel's God during a time of distress.

The exclusive competence of Yahweh in matters concerning sickness also comes through as an axiom of faith in the second exemplary passage here (Ezek. 13:17 ff), in which the prophet Ezekiel castigates the production and use of magic articles. These were offered by women—also called "prophetesses"—probably for the purpose of incantation procedures. Ezekiel chooses a cry of woe.

"Woe to the women who sew magic bands upon all wrists, and make veils for the heads of persons of every stature, in the hunt for souls!" This is a trespass into God's privilege. "You have profaned me among my people for handfuls of barley and for pieces of bread, putting to death persons who should not die and keeping alive persons who should not live." The following word of threat announces Yahweh's intervention: "Wherefore thus says the Lord God: Behold, I am against your magic bands with which you hunt the souls, and I will tear them from your arms; and I will let the souls that you hunt go free like birds. Your veils also I will tear off, and deliver my people out of your hand, and they shall be no more in your hand as prey; and you shall know that I am the Lord." The path already embarked upon is here condemned and threatened as a "profanation" (13:19) in a way different than in the Wisdom discussion concerning the correct path out of sickness.

A whole series of passages with varying content falls under the second aspect, that of figurative, metaphorically prophetic usage. Prophetic pronouncements of disaster often employ images of divinely sent epidemics and plagues; this is probably grounded in the fact that this is an old, and to a certain extent official, motif of sacral-legal sanctions and curses (Deut. 32; 2 Sam. 24; Amos 4:10; Hos. 5:12; 13:14). Apparently even on a collective level—and perhaps primarily there—that rigid course of action was also valid: pestilences are God's punishment; penitence leads to liberation and healing. In any case, the prophets reject this dogmatic schema as useless, even though it appeared valid to their contemporaries. This "cheap" path is excluded from now on, a path Hosea cites: "Come, let us return to the Lord; for he has torn, that he may heal us; he has stricken, and he will bind us up. After two days he will revive us; on the third day he will raise us up, that we may live before him" (Hos. 6:1). Isaiah refers to the same thing: "lest they (the people) turn and be healed" (6:10).

The transferral of the case of illness onto the present situation of the people as a whole (Isa. 1:5 f; 10:18; Jer. 30:12 ff) or onto the future disaster (e.g., Ezek. 30:21 ff) is more frequent, and again it is Yahweh's personal blow that causes these wounds. The transferral onto the situation of the prophet himself, on the other hand, as in Jeremiah 17:14, and probably also Isaiah 52:13 ff, is more isolated.

The third aspect, the absence of sickness, is found for the most part in later prophecy. An example is the pseudo-Isaiah passage in Isaiah 33:24, which reaches a climax as the conclusion of a future prophecy: "And no inhabitant will say, 'I am sick'; the people who dwell there will be forgiven their iniquity" (cf. 19:22). Thus we can say that the employment of the image of the sick person as a paradigm of God's actions is common to the prophets. It is, as it were, a cause-effect sequence, and thus a model encompassing the following points (among others): Yahweh intervenes directly in human life; his actions display the characteristics either of punishment or of healing; man is put into a place where guilt becomes punishment for him, and healing becomes salvation.

This network of associations is based, of course, on the paradigm of sickness the prophets had before them, a paradigm worked out by cultic-legal theology and theological Wisdom ethics. Nonetheless they dismember it even as they embrace it, employ some detail as a partial piece, and thus illuminate it anew with their configuration of reprimand-threat-salvation pronouncement. Thus Jeremiah, for example, and his tradition, develop the motif of the "incurable wound" (e.g., 30:12 f) as a sign of inescapable disaster. This, however, dissolves the image of the actual situation of the sick person. It becomes a parable of divine action and serves to concretize the recognition that

Yahweh's relationship to his people and its members has reached
a crisis.

5. Theological Statements

Several confessional statements—statements not just limited to cases of illness—attempt to articulate the sick person's
relationship to God. They do, however, refer primarily to cases
of illness, and to that extent, probably arose out of the theological
reflection on the typical situation and life crisis of the sick person.
We are speaking of that largely two-part formulation that
associates life and death, being struck and being healed as God's
actions, and in that it was very likely—as wide distribution
suggests—the model of confessional statements for the prophets.

The confessional statement, the so-called sovereignty
formulation, appears in various guises in an approximate
chronological sequence. In 2 Kings 5:7: the Israelite king reacts
to the presumption of a leprosy healing with the indignant cry:
"Am I God, to kill and to make alive" (*hiphil*-forms). In Hosea 6:1
in the dictum critically cited by Hosea concerning the
community which is ready for atonement: "Come, let us return
to the Lord; for he has torn, that he may heal us; he has stricken,
and he will bind us up. . . ." In Deuteronomy 32:39 f in the
so-called song of Moses, a prophetic text: "See now that I, even I,
am he, and there is no god beside me; I kill (*hiphil*) and I make
alive (*piel*); I wound and I heal; and there is none that can deliver
out of my hand." In 1 Samuel 2:6, the thanksgiving psalm of
Hannah: "The Lord kills (*hiphil*) and brings to life (*piel*); he
brings down to Sheol and raises (*hiphil*). The Lord makes poor
and makes rich; he brings low (*hiphil*), he also exalts (*piel*). In Job
5:18 f in Eliphaz' advice to Job: "For he wounds, but he binds up;
he smites, but his hands heal. He will deliver you from six
troubles; in seven there shall no evil touch you. . . ." Finally,
probably the most important confessional statement in our
context, a redactional (Deut.) addition in Exodus 15:26 (the
narrative of the "bitter fountain" of Marah): "For I am the Lord,
your healer." The customary translation of the final words is

misleading: "the Lord, your physician," because there were no physicians in Israel in the modern sense; no physicians besides wound surgeons and "patchers," until late in the Old Testament period. In this context it is highly significant that in the Canaanite environs the Ugarit equivalent (*rapi ' u*, "physician, healer, savior") was a title of honor for living kings such as Epitheton of the god Baal,[62] a title that Exodus 15 wrests from this deity and claims for Yahweh alone.[63]

This confession, whose stylized form (participial hymn style, polarity, I-statements, negations) attests to its distribution and significance, expresses the following important theological aspects of the interpretation of illness:

(1) *Yahweh's exclusive responsibility*

This formulation represents Yahweh's exclusive responsibility, as opposed to all other magical, demonic and also medical ideas about the origin of sickness, not only as regards the cause, but also the healing of sickness; it does this without qualification. One need only recall the strongly emphasized and exposed "I" (I, I alone am he) in Deuteronomy 32:39 and Exodus 15:26. This axiom probably originated on the basis of the first commandment (Exod. 20:2 f par).

(2) *The totality of Yahweh's power over life*

According to the stylistic law of "merism", this formulation encompasses all phenomena between "living" and "dying," and to that extent traces all sickness directly back to Yahweh's intervention: the "leprosy" of the Damascene, the childlessness of Hannah, Job's sickness, the Egyptian plagues, pestilence—"it is he who has done us this great harm, it happened to us not by chance" (in the sense of 1 Sam. 6:9).

(3) *The perpetual dependency of all life on Yahweh*

If life hangs in the balance between God's actions toward life and God's actions toward death, and if sickness is accordingly a crisis of balance which can only be resolved by opposing powers issuing from Yahweh, then man's existence remains continually suspended, held up above the abyss, or in the words of the statement of sovereignty: in Yahweh's hand (Deut. Hos. Job). The hovering, timeless hymnic style expresses the inalterable nature of this state of affairs. Thus it is, and thus will it always be!

This confession, appearing as Yahweh's self-revelation, as a hymnic predication and doxology, as a theoretical definition of the deity ('elohim 2 Kings 5:7), and as a polemical thesis, is in every case a final theological postulation about sickness. Old Testament reflection on this topic peaks, as it were, in this confession. In it, the Old Testament statements concerning sickness we have here sketched are in agreement and find a common denominator. The theological tension contained in this pointed formulation steps into a crass light if, in conclusion, one compares a reproduction of a roll-seal from Ur (about 2200 B.C.) (p. 68).[64]

Two scenes are juxtaposed. In the first a winged demon holds down two helpless human figures and the feet of a bird of prey tramples on a third. A sickness demon is tyrannizing men. The second shows the sun god, recognizable by his light-rays, before whom that sickness demon's helper is led. Sickness and healing thus depend on different powers, and are dependent upon the play and struggle of divine powers against one another. According to the Old Testament there is only one power responsible: sickness and healing are personalized in a special way as forms of action and manifestations of Yahweh's presence with his people.

III. Particular Cases of Sickness—Concretizations

1. "Leprosy"

The problem of what was traditionally called leprosy can, for the most part, be considered clarified, particularly after several

Reproduction of a cylinder-seal from Ur, third millenium. From O. Keel, *Die Welt der altorientalischen Bildsymbolik und das Alte Testament*, p. 68, Nr. 90a. Copyright Benziger Verlag, Zürich, Köln, 1972, used with permission.

recent medical-historical investigations—most notably by E. V. Hulse.[65] This is the sickness that in the Bible is called ṣara ' at in Hebrew and *lepra* in Greek and that plays such a central role in both testaments. According to these investigations we can be reasonably certain that (1) the biblical leprosy *(ṣara ' at, lepra)* has nothing to do with the sickness called leprosy by modern medicine which was discovered by the physician G. H. A. Hansen in 1868. During antiquity this disease was known in India and was probably first brought into the Near East by the troops of Alexander the Great. Earlier evidence for the ancient Near East cannot be found in spite of comprehensive investigations of skulls, on which leprosy leaves its traces. The imported sickness was called *elephas* (elephantiasis) by the Greeks. Not until the Middle Ages was *lepra* (previously known approximately as "scaly white rash") equated with *elephantiasis*, first documented by the Arabian physician John of Damascus (777-857). Both terms became synonymous, an event which up to the present has had scandalous consequences: under Christian influence the biblical contempt of "lepers" was transferred to those sick with actual leprosy. This is why the World Health Organization as well as many states saw themselves forced to oppose the use of the term leprosy in order to check the inhumane consequences for those sick with leprosy.[66] We can also be reasonably certain (2) that the disease called ṣara ' at in the Old Testament—astutely and appropriately observed as regards etymology and diagnosis as "wasp sting"[67]—as well as the New Testament *lepra*, encompasses in all the Old Testament passages a group of diseases modern medicine can identify. On the basis of the extremely useful, and by no means obsolete, descriptions and differentiations, these become recognizable as psoriasis (scaliness), and occasionally as favus or vitiligo, in addition to some less clear-cut skin diseases with similar symptoms (eczema, erysipelas, growths, rashes). Psoriasis is a chronic, noninfectious skin disease characterized by well-marked, lightly raised red spots of various sizes, covered with dry, gray-white or silver scales. The infected places itch, and if they are scratched, the scales come off as flakes and reveal a moist, reddish surface with tiny bleeding spots—like insect bites.[68] Vitiligo, or favus, is, from a medicinal point of view, a much more dangerous disease affecting the skin of the head or the hair itself and causing a yellow encrustation around the individual hairs. It affects the deeper levels of the skin, causes a loss of hair and leaves behind a slick, shiny, thin, white spot. According to Leviticus 13:29-37, favus is primarily considered to be a form of ṣara ' at, although one can still see that a particular disease is probably meant here (Hebrew neteq).

The Old Testament presents the symptoms of psoriasis-ṣara ' at by means of the customary comparison "(flaky, not white) as snow" (Exod. 4:6; Num. 12:10b; 2 Kings 5:27), with reference to the flakelike scales. It also uses the singular comparison—although, according to Hulse, a perfectly appropriate one—of the diseased places on the skin with a miscarriage (Num. 12:12), and gives detailed diagnoses in Leviticus 13 which put the priest in a position to differentiate ṣara ' at from other diseases that are similar but not cultically impure. The criteria are primarily silver scales, a flesh-colored underlayer, and white-powdered, non-colored hair on the infected spots. The Septuagint and the New Testament thus appropriately translate ṣara ' at as lepra (the "white-scaled" disease): lepsis, "scale," and lepo, to peel or scale; both describe the characteristics of psoriasis (see B.III.2).

The Old Testament documentation, in spite of its historically varying order, gives in general a fairly accurate acount of the situation of the "leper," or person with a skin disease.

Numbers 12 tells about Miriam's sudden illness. She became leprous "as snow." Her appearance precipitates the request to Moses to pray for her so that she "not be as one dead, of whom the flesh is half consumed when he comes out of his mother's womb." Moses cries out to Yahweh and receives the answer that Miriam's case is like that of a woman spit on by her father and thus punished and publicly denounced. She should be "shamed" for seven days and be "shut up outside the camp"; only then—recovery is presupposed—can she again be accepted into the community of the "camp."

These archaic-sounding features, particularly the ideas and behavioral forms not otherwise known to the Old Testament, show how those in ancient Israel viewed this kind of case and how they acted towards it. Psoriasis-leprosy was considered to be a punishment and disgrace, and probably also a threat to life—as the comparison with the miscarriage suggests—but in any case an impurity of the highest order. A healing process mediated by intercession resulted above all in rites of re-integration. "Leprosy" was primarily a cultic-religious, i.e., a social, problem.

The element of admonition in Numbers 5:1 ff and Deuteronomy 24:8 makes it clear that people were inclined to keep a case of "leprosy" secret because of its serious consequences, or at least they tended to deal with it only reluctantly. Those around the sick person also were involved in a conflict of conscience.

It is difficult to say just when and how this skin disease in Israel acquired the significance later tradition ascribed to it. The randomness of the preserved Priestly material in Leviticus 12–15 concerning purity laws may be the reason this gravity became associated with psoriasis. In any case, Leviticus 13–14 presents the Priestly teaching necessary for differentiating between various skin and other surface diseases in order to recognize and evaluate a case of ṣara 'at as cultically impure. The seven sections in Leviticus 13:1-44 give the various examinations, criteria of differentiation, tests, and case descriptions that seemed to be necessary for this procedure.

> To be sure, the material . . . was hardly a totally unified structure from the very beginning, but rather, as shown by the details, it was the result of a growth process, in the course of which what seemed important concerning the topic of contamination by skin diseases and the necessary purifications measures, was written down and then completed by additional details.[69]

The significant chapter on purification, Leviticus 14, shows a number of rituals which grew in number in a step-by-step fashion; they all concern healing, but were hardly all practiced in reality. It probably just represented an accumulation of material concerning the topic before it was brought into the Priestly purification writings.[70]

Leviticus 13 is structured in such a way that suggestions for a normal case are given in an initial section (vv 2-4). If one suspects *ṣara ' at*-"leprosy," if one finds swellings, eruptions and spots on the skin, the person concerned is to be examined by the priest. Two symptoms are to be noted: (1) whether the hair coloring on the affected spot has changed to white (because of the falling away of scabs) and (2) whether the place appears to be deeper than the surrounding skin (probably after the crust was scratched away). If both symptoms obtain, then it is a *ṣara ' at*-sore. The priest is to declare the person cultically impure by speaking the appropriate words.

Verses 5-8 deal with the first sub-case. Both symtoms are only partly or not at all recognizable. The whitening of the hairs and the indentation cannot be ascertained. In that case the suspected "leper" is to be separated and then brought forth again after seven days. If the findings are the same, then the same procedure is to be repeated. If the sore is paler and has not spread further, then the sick person can be pronouncd pure. He is to wash himself and is then pure again. If, however, the priest finds that the sore has spread, he must be examined again.

A second sub-case is described in verses 9-17 which in a way is competing with the normal case (new introduction). Instead of the above-mentioned second symptom (skin indentation), another is named, namely the flesh-colored growth on the swelling. This is referring to the special form of the "old"[71] or "sleeping leprosy."[72] The findings here correspond to those of normal *ṣara ' at*, but not if the symptoms can be ascertained over the entire body (for example in the case of dermatitis or scarlet fever). In that case one is not dealing with biblical *ṣara ' at*. The sick person is cultically pure.

The third sub-case (vv 18-25) deals with *ṣara ' at* as the result of (healed over) abscesses. The scar is to be examined for the two main symptoms.

Burn wounds comprise a fourth special case (vv 24-28). Here, too, one is to come to a decision concerning the main symptoms.

A fifth new case is introduced in verses 29-37. These verses are concerned with a skin disease in the area of head or beard hair, which is distinguished from the normal case. The symptoms are a depression in the skin and gold-yellow coloration of the (thin) hair. This is *neteq* (their own term), or favus (scabies, or something similar). It is considered to be a parallel case with *ṣara ' at* (cf. Lev. 15:54, where both terms are introduced together).

The sixth case (vv. 38, 39), that of a simple white eruption (probably leucodermatosis) is to be differentiated from the *ṣara ' at* group.

A final (seventh) special case emerges in verses 40-44 by means of the differentiation between normal baldness of the head and head "leprosy," which appears on the baldness as a white-reddish spot and looks like body "leprosy." One is to proceed accordingly.[73]

We can only list here the complicated purification procedures concerning *ṣara ' at*-"leprosy" collected by Leviticus 14. After successful healing the patient is to submit to an examination by the priest. Purification rites follow first, then sacrificial acts (vv 2-3). The first of these involved the two-bird ritual, double washing of clothes, cutting of hair, washing of the body after a seven-day interval (vv 4-9).

The latter involved the guilt sacrifice, the blood and oil ritual, as well as the sacrificial trio of guilt-, food-, and burnt-offering (vv 10-20). In the case of poverty a reduction was possible (vv 21-31).

A noteworthy phenomenon is that a case of *ṣara ' at* could also appear on materials (13:47-59) and houses (14:34-53). In this transferral one sees the deeply rooted idea that surface injuries on both men and things were a particularly drastic manifestation of the numinous quality of disease; they were, so to speak, the port of entry for dangerous, super-natural powers. It was no accident that skin diseases were considered to be particularly volatile cases from the cultic and religious perspective. The medical side of things played only a subordinate role.[74]

We have already spoken about the social situation of the person sick with "leprosy" (I.2). It is graphically portrayed in Leviticus 13:45 f, but also in Numbers 12; 2 Kings 5, 7, and 15, as well as in the New Testament. Since people usually conjure up a false image of a person sick with leprosy, let us here cite a passage from a modern description of the disease psoriasis: ". . . incapable of rolling up one's sleeves and washing oneself publicly; avoid school, take part in no sports, and no vacation fun on the coast or on the sea; leaving behind traces of silvery scales at home and specks of blood on paper, and having to fear public looks—that is a horrible fate."[75]

In moderate zones, psoriasis has a frequency quota of 1 or 2 percent. Applied to ancient Israel, with an estimated total population of about one million in both states during the period of kings (Palestine probably could not support more than that), this would have amounted to approximately 10 to 20,000 cases. This would mean that in Samaria, for example, shortly before its destruction by Sargon II in 721 B.C., out of about 30,000 inhabitants approximately 300 people were affected by it (according to R. de Vaux).[76] Thus, in every larger town at least some people were "lepers," and the numbers make the relative frequency in the Old Testament documents seem plausible. Nonetheless, this arithmetic is not without problems, since it is probable that the disease occurs less frequently in warmer zones. Finally, we should also remember that ṣara ' at-favus would be much more dangerous to life and health. The Priestly theory of purity, with its thinking oriented to sacral contexts, also ascribes to these skin diseases on the whole (nega'ṣara ' at) a place closer to death than to life (B.III.2).

2. King Saul

According to tradition, King Saul suffered from depression or melancholy, or in any case, from some spiritual illness.[77] And indeed, judging from his spoken reactions, it appears to have been some sort of depression. When an evil spirit (1 Sam. 16:16; 18:10; 19:9) from Yahweh (16:14) came over him after the good Spirit of the Lord departed from him—as 1 Samuel 16:14 interprets it—he became terrified and frightened, acted occasionally like a prophet and "raved within his house" (18:10). Only when David played the lyre did the music appear to calm him down; things went better for him again, and he felt refreshed and well (16:23). The narrator says: "And the evil spirit departed from him." The texts do not offer us anything more concrete than that. The attempt at a kind of music therapy is interesting, a therapy which for a time apparently had the right effect. However, the image of the melancholy king found a secure place in the memory of later generations.

This gives us the opportunity to say something about the situation of a sick king in the ancient Near East. A ruler's sickness, no matter which cultural environment served as the backdrop, had to affect his social and sacral status and thus had consequences reaching deep into the political arena. Indeed, the welfare of the entire people was at stake—not just that of the dynasty—if its representative was marked by sickness. The Old Testament does not give us any explicit examples, aside from David's child (2 Sam. 12) and the "leprous" Uzziah (with special status! 2 Kings 15). However, the KRT-epic found in Ugarit treats precisely this problem and all its consequences for an old Canaanite royal house. To that extent it is a distant analogy to the writing about Job, where a similar problem is debated, albeit with an eye on different aspects, as one would expect. The late fragment found in Qumran with "Nabonid's Prayer" (4QOrNab) can contribute within the context of the legend and so-called epistle of Nebuchadnezzar in Daniel 3:31–4:34. This letter is on the whole still too unknown to research to permit anything more concrete to be determined.

3. Ezekiel

The peculiarities the tradition recounts to us from the life of the prophet Ezekiel have given rise to the question whether the striking appearance of this prophet does not go so far beyond the limit of what is normal that pathological causes should be sought. Among other well-known scholars, K. Jaspers has made a contribution to this investigation: "Der Prophet Ezechiel. Eine pathographische Studie" (1947).[78] The research interested in this question was influenced early by A. Klostermann's suggestion, published in 1877,[79] that Ezekiel 3–24 was the diary of a sick person suffering from paralysis. Indeed, because of repeated speech incapacity and paralysis of alternating sides of the body (Ezek. 4:4 ff) as a sign of "hemiplegia," this ailment was to be taken on the whole as catalepsy, prompted by internal, spiritual causes. Jaspers, on the other hand, as others before him,[80] understood the book as the report of an illness and sought to recognize the typical course of schizophrenia in it.

W. Zimmerli has quite correctly called attention to the questionable nature of the kind of textual investigation and evaluation. He has simultaneously shown how difficult it is to find the figure of the "historical" Ezekiel within the layered structure of the book as it has come down to us, and has shown that it is virtually impossible to gain a unified, well-defined picture of the sickness from the sum of material before us.[81]

To this we add the fact that precisely those appearances judged to be symptoms of illness stand variously in parts which have the distinct character of proclamation or demonstration: Symbolic acts (lying 390 days on the left, 40 days on the right side in order to "bear" the punisment for Israel's 390-year and Judah's 40-year guilt) and ritualistic acts (silence is a stage in the ritual of grief, 24:15 ff).[82] "All these characteristics of physical weakness, combined with the sensibility of a man seized by images and visages and forced to participate in the experience even in a physical sense, hardly suffice to determine a specific diagnosis of sickness for the prophet by using medical insights usually applied to a 'normal sick person.' " There remains only the possibility of an abnormal, or seemingly pathological, condition standing behind the "binding with cords" in 4:4 ff—and all this is too little to enable us to come to a clear, concrete understanding.[83]

4. The Suffering Servant (Isaiah Ch. 53)

The descriptions of the suffering of the Servant of God (' ebed Yahweh) in Deutero-Isaiah portray him as a "man of sorrows/pains" struck down by sickness. This figure stands at the center of the so-called suffering servant songs (Isa. 42:1-4; 49:1-6; 50:4-9; 52:13-53:12), in whom characteristics of this anonymous exile prophet himself become recognizable in an increasingly more distinct fashion.[84] His repulsive external appearance prompted his fellow men to despise, indeed to reject or forsake him (53:2 f). The text itself does not allow us to conclude that he was "leprous," as B. Duhm, who has separated out the texts mentioned above, suggested. The customary designation for that (ṣara ' at) is missing in Isaiah 53. One can certainly consider, however, whether he was not physically handicapped from a very early age. This might explain why his appearances no longer seemed human, but rather abnormal: "His appearance was so marred, beyond human semblance" (52:14). And: "For he grew up before him like a young plant, and like a root out of dry ground; he had no form or comeliness that we should look at him, and no beauty that we should desire him" (53:2). This was the reason for the piously motivated contempt: "We esteemed him stricken, smitten by God, and afflicted," "as one from whom men hide their faces he was despised, and we esteemed him not" (53:4, 3). This contempt by his fellow believers—if the allusions may be understood in this way—brought him even additional suffering. He is arrested by the Babylonian authorities (?), condemned, executed, and buried as a criminal (53:7 ff). The chain of his suffering ends in death.

The community expressing itself in Isaiah 53 realized only *post mortem* what the significance of this fate was. Isa. 52:12-53:13 portrays a heavenly legal assembly,[85] and the community's confessionlike testimony before this court describes the life course of the prophetic servant with elements of the penitential lament paradigm.[86] It also portrays the servant's unprecedented, singular elevation with metaphorically employed images of a restitution of salvation (53:10, if this difficult text is to be taken in this way[87]). This is why some of the portrayal's characteristics are stereotyped, and why the servant thus becomes a kind of prototype of sufferers in general. To that extent any search for possible symptoms of a specific illness does not appear to be particularly promising. Certain aspects of human suffering, however, are very likely united in this passion portrayal and are meshed together into a picture that lets us recognize its meaning in that interweaving of guilt-punishment-suffering-death, a meaning transcending all our powers of imagination: "Surely he has borne our griefs/sicknesses, and carried our sorrows/pains . . . but he was wounded for our transgressions, he was bruised for our iniquities; upon him was the chastisement that made us whole" (53:4).[88]

5. The Case of Job

The attempt to diagnose Job's sickness is, in reality, futile, since he is a fictional case, a pedagogical example, and a model both in the prose narrative (1–2; 42) and in the poetic dialogue. We can only attempt this in a limited fashion by asking how the narrator and poet understood Job's severe physical suffering. This discussion suffers from the excessive naïveté with which one assumes the Wisdom tradition authors understood sicknesses which were clearly defined and diagnosable. The only question appearing interesting (whether it was leprosy or not) was additionally burdened with the entire weight of the *ṣara ' at* problem. If we are permitted (according to III.1) to relinquish this excessive burden in the sense of "leprosy"-lepra, then not very much remains in the way of concrete details. There is, however, apparently enough to characterize the situation of a person afflicted with a severe illness, a situation to which everyone had access as a result of his own experience. It could thus function as the object of a certain teaching and become the occasion for extensive reflection.

According to the story about the pious sufferer Job, the illness was by definition not dangerous to life—"Only spare his life"—and "afflicted Job with loathesome sores from the sole of his foot to the crown of his head" (*šᵉḥî*). According to Leviticus 13:18-23, this can only be considered the prerequisite and disposition for the possible emergence of the "leprous" illness. The same designation is used in the description of Hezekiah's illness (2 Kings 20:7; Isa. 38:21) and probably also for the illness of Nabonid standing behind Daniel 4 and transmitted in the extra-canonical Qumran fragment: "Struck down with a loathesome sore by command of the highest God."[89] We read that Job "took a potsherd with which to scrape himself, and sat among the ashes" (2:8). The Greek translation explains further that it was a refuse heap "outside the city" (it imagines Job to be living in a city), the *mezbele* of Syrian-Palestinian locales. A. Musil remarks concerning this: "If the illness lasts any longer, then his relatives take him out during the dry season to the high, wall-like refuse heap outside the locale, erect a shade roof over him by securing a roof on four poles, and here he lies often entire days and nights. From here he looks out on the surrounding fields, on the village, and his eyes wander out over the wide, open steppes and desert . . ." (Arabia Petraea III).[90] Again, it is the image offered by the Septuagint. The Hebraic text only wishes to relate that Job bends into the "dust and ashes" under the blows that have afflicted him (42:6).

The narrator traces the illness back to a blow delivered by the heavenly prosecutor, Satan, with permission from the highest source for the purpose of testing Job's piety. The prosecutor is of the opinion that health and life are the most important possessions in Job's eyes, possessions he tries to maintain by means of his piety. "Skin for skin! All that a man has he will give for his life. But put forth thy hand now, and touch his bone and his flesh" (2:4 f). Job passes this test and holds unswervingly to his faith: "Shall we receive good at the hand of God, and shall we not receive evil?" (2:10). He reacts as Yahweh predicted and thus becomes a model for wisdom, faith and life which is granted a happy ending.

Job finds healing, compensation and rehabilitation. The first of these is mentioned only in passing, together with the restitution according to the ancient Israelite compensation principle of a double amount—Job appears to be one whom God wronged.[91] It also uses the politically coined phrase "to restore one's fortunes" (*šūb š'būt*), because Job's case is considered to be a theo-political one in which God's justice is manifested. The third aspect of his restoration acquires particular significance. "Then came to him all his brothers and sisters and all who had known him before, and ate bread with him in his house; and they showed him sympathy and comforted him for all the evil that the Lord had brought upon him; and each of them gave him a piece of money *(qesitah)* and a ring of gold" (42:11). The belated relatives' oft-maligned behavior may well have given rise to various literary-critical operations,[92] but it appears to fit better into the plot progression than previously thought. It is not, after all, a matter of a belated consolation visit (in the sense of the modern bourgeois custom), but rather of the reintegration into the community effected by means of that visit. This rehabilitation of the recovered person was normally realized by means of cultic rituals, particularly the celebration of a cultic meal. Since the sacrifice precedes all this (42:7), we are directed to the second part of the restitution procedure; in this case it occurs as a common meal within the family circle. With that the sick person steps back into life, and he dies an old man, full of days (42:17).

We encounter a completely different Job in the dialogues (3–42). The poet uncovers the inner side of suffering here, and in a dramatic treatment of the situation takes a certain problem as his theme. This problem is the theme of the ancient oriental genre concerned with the "suffering righteous person." Three main works can be named: *Ludlul bēl nēmeqi* ("I will praise the Lord of wisdom"), the report version of the suffering righteous people (Louvre-Version) and the Sumerian poetical work on Job ("Man and his God"). In the Job dialogue, however, it is in the final analysis a matter of the deeper dimensions of the Yahweh faith. What is expressed here in a "dramatized lament" (C. Westermann[93]) and in various forms of speech and speech directions, what is actually under discussion along these endlessly long, reflective paths, is the question prompted by illness: How is one to behave in this kind of situation?[94] With Job it is expressed as curse lament, penitential lament, lament against enemies, and accusation; with the friends it is expressed as teaching, advice, admonition and reprimand. In Job's words it becomes an address and challenge to God with growing intensity from the very beginning. It is a practical problem, the question concerning the path *(derek)*, or exit, out of the dilemma and labyrinth of suffering. According to our own presuppositions, this life question might be separated into the theoretical question of what has happened, ordering and evaluating the experience of suffering within the traditional system of order; and this could be done with the aid of familiar categories of comprehension so that a recognizable network of associations could emerge and understanding could become possible. In this context, the friends represent that traditional thought filter that follows the logical line from sickness to guilt according to firmly established legal analogies; traditional thought thus thinks of punishment, something which in its own turn, as divine punishment, stands under the formal law of unerring correctness. All the friends' remarks in all stages of the discussion are determined by this basic line, all the way to the assumptions emerging from this thought structure as consequence and postulate.

The Job of the dialogue is not able simply to accept this thought model for his own case. To be sure, he basically knows and agrees with the first premise underlying this schema: God is the originator of suffering. But he is not able to accept the other premise in his own case: Suffering is just punishment for guilt; or: God punishes justly. The dimensions of an experience of suffering cannot be measured with the standard of the dogmatic schema. This is why dissent emerges concerning the other, practical aspect of the problem, the question concerning the appropriate behavior in the face of illness. We have already seen in an earlier section which possibilities and alternatives are basically available in such a situation. The customary behavior always offered by cult and pastoral care within the Yahweh faith, and also advised by the friends, was what we may call "penitential grief," for want of an adequate term in Hebrew; F. Horst calls this "sacral confession." Practically, this means a public confession of guilt and an acceptance of suffering as punishment. "The confession consisting in *confessio* and doxology offers the person submitting to it the possibility of experiencing a *restitutio* from God."[95] This is precisely what Job is not prepared to do, since, to his knowledge, he has no guilt to confess. The friends never tire, all the way up to Elihu's speech (33), of propagating this clear path sanctioned in their own eyes by tradition. They do not, however, mention that a person embarks upon this prescribed path under the pressure of hypocrisy, among other things, and that this way back *(šûb)* conceals an unreasonable demand made of God—as the prophets well know (e.g. Hos. 6:1-3). And above all, they do not mention that Job has long attempted to pursue other paths. Thus the impression arises that the friends remain all the more in one place the longer the discussion lasts, while Job—briefly held back only by Elihu—goes about seeking other ways of drawing closer to God.

With increasing intensity Job seeks a way out in a direct confrontation with God. Although he holds fast here in a quite traditional manner to God's so-called "healing monopoly" (J. Hempel), he nonetheless traverses completely new paths as far as his own case is concerned.

He does not seek contact on the path of penitential lament, but rather—expressed in cultic imagery—along the path of a legal quest. He wants a sacral-legal proceeding in order to attain a divine judgment in his own case. He feels deprived of his rights, his fundamental right to life, robbed by God; indeed, robbed unjustifiably and without reason. Thus he seeks to bring God before the limitations of a court of law, knowing full well and in sheer despair what a monstrous and virtually insane demand that is. This, however, is how those passages in his speeches are to be understood in which he cries out for a divine judgment over God. What is initially a wish:

> Even now, behold, my witness is in heaven,
> and he that vouches for me is on high.
> My friends scorn me;
> my eye pours out tears to God,
> that he would maintain the right of a man with God,
> like that of a man with his neighbor (16:19-21)

> and:

> Oh that my words were written!
> Oh that they were inscribed in a book!
> Oh that with an iron pen and lead
> they were graven in the rock for ever!
> For I know that my Redeemer/Vindicator lives . . . .
> (19:23 f)[96]

becomes a direct address at the end of the purification oath already taken over as the first stage of the divine court proceeding (29–31):

Oh, that I had one to hear me!
(Here is my signature! let the
Almighty answer me!)
Oh, that I had the indictment
    written by my adversary!
Surely I would carry it on my shoulder;
I would bind it on me as a crown;
I would give him an account of all my steps;
like a prince I would approach him. (31:35-37)

These wishes and the direct address are successful. Yahweh
answers Job from the whirlwind, and his advent properly
realigns the respective positions. Job goes back to his place
(40:3 ff; 42:1 ff). The lock is opened from the outside, and Job
leaves justified and healed.

Along these prodigious reflective paths[97] traversed by Job,
the poet has ample opportunity to discuss wisdom-illness
experiences, including accumulated educational content such as
his own experiences in illness; some of these concern our topic
here and will now be discussed. We have already spoken above
about the social study in chapter 19, as well as about the
behavioral paradigm in chapter 33. We can here add the
"portrayal of misery" which itself has been added as a sketch to
the past-present schema of the purification oath; it offers
considerable insight also into corresponding portrayals in the
psalms. Enemies are pressuring the sick person:

Because God has loosed my cord
    and humbled me,
they have cast off restraint in my presence.
On my right hand the rabble rise,
they drive me forth,
they cast up against me their ways of destruction.
                                            (30:11-12)

Pain is added to this: "The night racks my bones" (30:17). These
make him struggle against God.

God has cast me into the mire,
and I have become like dust and ashes. (30:19)

Thou hast turned cruel to me;
with the might of thy hand thou
does persecute me. . . .
Yea, I know that thou wilt bring me to death,
and to the house appointed for all living.

(30:21 ff)

At the conclusion stands the painful and bitter mention of his penitence—now either taken over by him or ascribed to him by convention (cf. 16:15 ff):

I go about blackened, but not by the sun;
I stand up in the assembly, and cry for help.
I am a brother of jackals,
and a companion of ostriches.
My skin turns black and falls from me,
and my bones burn with heat.
My lyre is turned to mourning,
and my pipe to the voice of those who weep.

(30:28 ff)

The entire lament paradigm is collected here.

Chapter 18 describes the effect of a pestilence, called the "first-born of death", within the context of a typological portrayal of the godless. It catches man like a hidden trap, chases him like an animal of prey, and is "ready for his stumbling" (18:12). His skin and limbs are consumed, and he is brought to the "king of terrors," death. But not even that is enough! His memory and name perish, brimstone is scattered upon his tent, and he is finally thrust into darkness. With "no offspring or descendant among his people," he, the god-less one, dies the final death.

Here and there we find passages dealing with the world of the dead, the land of no return which makes everyone equal (3:17 ff; 21:23 ff) and also moving laments about the sick person's proximity to death (e.g., 17:11 ff, II.2).

The ideas offered in chapter 10 concerning the formation of the child in the mother's womb are interesting from a medical-historical perspective; these ideas are surprising in view of the general ignorance of physiological processes:

Thy hands fashioned and made me;
and now thou dost turn about and destroy me.
Remember that thou hast made me of clay;
and wilt thou turn me to dust again?
Didst thou not pour me out like milk
    and curdle me like cheese?
Thou didst clothe me with skin and flesh,
and knit me together with bones and sinews.
Thou has granted me life and steadfast love;
and thy care has preserved my spirit.

(10:8-12)[98]

The sea of ideas can hardly be exhausted. Nonetheless, as the final result of this colossal struggle, there remains the breakthrough of a new path out of the distress of illness, a path leading out because it is prepared from the outside and broken "breach upon breach" (16:14).

IV. Preliminary Steps Toward an Old Testament Interpretation of Sickness—Summary

A portrayal of the Old Testament understanding of sickness ordered according to the various epochs proves to be impossible. The sources do not allow this. But even if adequate sources stood at our disposal, one would have to ask whether it is really probable that in ancient Israel at any given time only one, or few, or even any clearly identifiable interpretation of sickness at all ever dominated. Certainly one must keep in mind that in secluded communities, and in clearly defined cultural circles, unified views of the world and of life determined thought and action; thus at certain times the one or the other understanding of sickness and healing was the dominant one. However, we lack precisely those sources that would enable us to draw the corresonding boundaries and to differentiate adequately between the epochs and societies. One simply cannot, on the given foundation, offer a portrayal of the understanding of sickness during the patriarchal period, for example, or for the royal court in Jerusalem during the Assyrian period, or for the holy places out in the country before Josiah's reform. Again: Even if there were a unified, dominant, as it were, an official and recognized theology in the circles mentioned, there is no traversable path allowing us to find even a theology of sickness within the reconstructed schematic framework of such broader interpretations; one is not able to draw out the conceptual lines anthropologically and thus come up with an image. Perhaps this kind of synthesis must be examined, but for the topic to be discussed here it cannot come into question.

What a summary can accomplish, however, is this: The individual results of intellectual efforts concerning the phenomenon of sickness, marked and proven as such, as they emerged in Israel at various times and under various conditions, should be collected and chronologically ordered and juxtaposed. This procedure has the advantage that the content can be presented as the result of various experiences lying in the past in which the relevant spiritual and religious factors participate; and further, that the connecting lines inevitably attempted between the individual data become recognizable as historical developments or synoptic considerations; and finally, that the impulses and motives of the entire intellectual process concerning the phenomenon of sickness—at least to the extent they can be recognized in traces in the Old Testament—become transparent.

1. The Patriarchal Faith in God

The oldest statements presumably come from the partriarchal period. To be sure, they are not concerned with sickness in the real sense. In one case, it is a matter of an injury (a hip out of joint, Gen. 32), in another, of a woman's infertility. Both cases fit into the patriarchal milieu. The roots of the story about Jacob's struggle with the angel at Jabbok probably reach back into the patriarchal period, in whose nomadic society the question concerning the son and heir, or posterity, also played a central role. Both cases offered the occasion for fundamental truth statements. Genesis 32 reflects a learning process in which the patriarch Jacob is led to understand the numinous assault on his existence as one of the ways the El-deity—whom he is to worship—acts. In the course of time—without its being specifically predictable—this deity is then identified with his previous God, then with Yahweh, according to the narrative's further levels of meaning.

The stages of the cognitive process still clearly visible show that the experience of the presence of a (of this) God in a clinch with man—a presence physically near, threatening to life and yet with the character of blessing—was new as well as painful. What is treated and taught here is confirmed in the other passages. In the various places where the infertility motif occurs in the patriarchal legends, it is implicitly or explicitly associated with the knowledge that it is the personally experienced God who is responsible, as the God of the clan, for protection and blessing. This is the God who "closed all the wombs of the house of Abimelech" and then, interceding again, "healed" them (Gen. 20:17 f; 16:2); the God Jacob means when he says: "Am I in the place of God, who has withheld from you the fruit of the womb?" (Gen. 30:2); the God who "afflicted Pharaoh" (Gen. 12:17) and who, in any case, is the subject of the action here, even though in a warning, punishing fashion. In both cases the action of sickness and healing takes place on representative persons, exponents of their families, clans, or people. The stories about the matriarchs (the name interpretation in Gen. 29:31 f is exemplary), as well as the Hannah narrative in 1 Samuel 1f, show that the patriarchal religion, geared for a personal partnership between the patriarch and his God,[99] could also become a direct relationship, characteristically mediated by the holy place itself, for personally affected individual people, namely the women.

2. The Fundamental Confession: "Yahweh, Your Savior"

In the early Israelite texts which presumably originated in the epoch of the land acquisition and judges, the perspective expands to include the people of Israel, and sickness appears, above all, in collective aspects such as pestilence or plague.

Two viewpoints here are of significance for a theological anthropology. First of all, the sickness phenomena appear as punishment intended and sent by the deity for transgressions against the relationship of loyalty presupposed between Yahweh and his people. The pestilence in Numbers 25, the plague of snakes in Numbers 21, and also Miriam's leprosy in Numbers 12, count as punishments for worshiping foreign gods. In Miriam's case, it occurs after Yahweh has withdrawn and is compared with the father's denunciation of his daughter as a publicly appropriate punishment. Manifestations of sickness are thus signs of divine wrath, ultimate warnings; they are divine sanctions and as such are indicators of the condition of the relationship to God. To that extent, they are of general and public interest in each particular representative case, as one can see in Miriam's case. In a reverse manner, standard, probably pre-deuteronomic, and perhaps quite old, texts associate the absence of health impairments, blessing, fertility, and health with an intact, sound relationship with God. "You shall serve the Lord your God, and he will bless your bread and your water; and he will take sickness away from the midst of you. None shall cast her young or be barren in your land; he will fulfill the number of your days" (Exod. 23:25 f). Yahweh's presence among the people holding to him means life, health, salvation—shalom—while this same presence in another instance can precipitate the effects of curse (cf. the old curse text in Deut. 28:16 ff), as well as the narrative about the ark in 1 Sam. 5 and 6).

On the other hand, the context of sickness appears to have been exposed, theologically, to increasingly strong conflicts emerging from the fact that, in Israel's immediate environment, other views concerning sickness were dominant and other, probably more impressive, practices in the treatment of sickness were in vogue. The practice of healing very early became a *status confessionis* of the Yahweh faith in the face of Canaanite daily life. It immediately becomes clear that boundaries broke down here, even if we will probably never succeed in uncovering boundary transgressions in this area. The path to healing is, for Numbers 12 and 21, naturally the path back to Yahweh via the confession "We have sinned." But the medicinal snake symbol appears already in Numbers 21:4 ff, still innocently taken as Yahweh's beneficial gift, as a remedy against snake bite; only in the context of indigenous fertility cults is it considered dangerous and abolished at the end of the eighth century during the reign of Hezekiah (2 Kings 18:4). The confessional statement in Exodus 15:26 is a documentation of the very likely tedious struggle in this area, and one notices the reflection of a taxing, difficult victory in the statement. It grants to Yahweh alone, in a polemical sense, the predication of "savior," a saving God, *rofe* ' (as a participle: "The one healing you"). According to Canaanite-Ugaritic documents, this predication was also attributed to the god Baal (as an ancient Canaanite royal title[100]) in the form of a word also used in Hebrew: *rapi* ' *u*. The sovereignty with which the ark narrative plays with this faith statement is incomparable; it finally brings the naïve Philistines themselves to a recognition of Yahweh's *solus* within the context of their suffering. It appears safe to say that sickness is to be traced back to God's hand and that "what happened to us" was no accident (1 Sam. 6:9).

3. Views Concerning the Sickness and Healing of a People and of an Individual

An overview of the pertinent texts from the period of kings leads to the observation that the problem of sickness is treated convergently in the affected areas and by the authorities concerned with it; this is the case to the extent that the individual person and his suffering become increasingly more visible. This does not mean that the views previously acquired and represented concerning the God-relatedness and communal character of sickness are suspended. On the contrary, the prophets vehemently take up these themes. Nonetheless, the documents focus increasingly on the individual aspects of sickness; indeed, on the typical, characteristic associative signs, though not on individual illnesses or cases.

Wisdom is the first area of sickness interpretation we can mention. The intellectual endeavors based on practical life experience, and reflecting on associations manifest in that experience, endeavors called "Wisdom," are primarily concerned with the nature and origin of man. The fundamental determination of man, documented within the framework of primeval history in Genesis 2, is traced back to Wisdom: "Then the Lord God formed man of dust from the ground, and breathed into his nostrils the breath of life, and man became a living being" (2:7). If God had not found it necessary to undertake corrections on the original model because of the course of human history, then this model-image would hardly allow room for physiological causes of sickness—unless it were the physical building material ("dust, ground"), injuries from external sources (the perpetually dominating image of sickness), or, above all, the withdrawal of life breath. To be sure, within the context of the guilt-punishment narrative of the so-called "fall," there is no mention of sickness; there is considerable talk, however, of curselike burdens and aggravations characterizing human existence from that point on: the woman's pain in childbearing, tiresome aggravations and torments for man during the pursuit of the general life supports, and God-willed diminution of life. The afflictions of daily life find their basis precisely here.

If we are permitted to place the Yahwistic primal history at the beginning of the period of kings, then the Job narrative would probably stand at the end. Here, too, an individual case is under question, though not, to be sure, that of the anonymous first man, but rather an individual man mentioned by name, but thought of as a model in which the typical situation of sickness is to be demonstrated. The "heavenly host" itself lingers "invisibly around the sick person's bed, his suffering becomes a theater play for the angels, the manifestation of God in his creature, a creature to which his eyes carefully direct themselves as if in justification of his own concerns" (J. G. von Herder).[101] These are two models of Wisdom anthropology, from the beginning and waning period of kings, marking the process of individualization.

Second, the prophets generally stand as representatives and messengers of their God to Israel as an entire people, even though in the early period they direct themselves to the kings in the execution of their mandates, and later to a wide variety of groups, classes, and authorities. This means—aside from exceptions—that the prophet was concerned with sickness and healing in a three-fold manner: as an oracular authority for a diagnosis, primarily for kings and representative persons; as a critic of customary manners of treatment, for example, by means of authorities alien to Yahweh such as Baal of Ekron; and as proclaimers of divine judgment which is to come in the form of plagues and pestilence. All three aspects are united in the Elijah narrative in 2 Kings 1, and all three receive independent portrayals from the individual prophets (e.g. Hos. 6; Amos 4; Ezek. 13). It is significant that the prophets, too, take note of and mention the individual case in their own way within the framework of their mandate. The case of the sick person, i.e., of the person smitten and disciplined by God, becomes for them a parable for the Yahweh people's religious as well as political misery. "Why will you still be smitten, that you continue to rebel? The whole head is sick, and the whole heart faint. From the sole of the foot even to the head, there is no soundness in it, but bruises and sores and bleeding wounds; they are not pressed out, or bound up, or softened with oil. Your country lies desolate." That is how Isaiah puts it in the year 701 B.C. when only Jerusalem was left "like a booth in a vineyard, like a lodge in a cucumber field" (1:5 ff). The sick person does not notice what ails him. Since he does not react, healing is not possible (6:10). It is also significant that the prophets' own suffering, be it spiritual or physical, becomes thematic for them. Thus Jeremiah cries out for healing (17:14), Ezekiel suffers peculiar symbolic happenings, and Deutero-Isaiah's suffering servant consummates his life in representative suffering (Isa. 53). Here, too, an individual's fate becomes transparent for the interpretation of the phenomenon of sickness.

Third, holy places and priests were already working during

the period of kings on a behavioral paradigm for sickness. In any case, the priestly traditions, which are certainly preexilic in their oldest strata, allow us to conclude this. Examples are the leprosy Torah in Leviticus 13–14 (together with the admonitions in Deut. 24:8 f and Num. 5:1 ff), or the blessing-curse schema in Deuteronomy 28 and Leviticus 26, and above all the temple document in 1 Kings 8, in verses 37-40. Interestingly, and typical for the development we need to be observing here, the individual case is worked into the community action during outbreaks of pestilence or similar ocurrences: "If there is famine in the land, if there is pestilence or blight or mildew or locust or caterpillar; if their enemy besieges them in any of their cities; whatever plague, whatever sickness there is; whatever prayer, whatever supplication is made by any man or by all thy people Israel, each knowing the affliction of his own heart and stretching out his hands toward this house, then hear thou in heaven thy dwelling place, and forgive, and act, and render to each whose heart thou knowest, according to all his ways. . . ." The sequence of action reflects the path that, according to the theological temple documents, is to be traversed by the sick person on his way to recovery. The individual stages are known only from post-exilic texts (Ps. 107; Job 33).

Several psalms could possibly illuminate, from the perspective of the persons affected, the inner side of an illness liturgy throwing itself into relief, but the texts in question cannot be chronologically fixed. Nonetheless, it appears possible that perhaps Psalm 6, 30, and 41, and Isaiah 38 already belong to the preexilic period. In any case, Jeremiah's lamentations and Isaiah 53 prove that the lament paradigm already existed at the beginning as well as the end of the exilic period.

From the circle of deuteronomic-deuteronomistic theology, finally, we have several documents showing that the reflection on the fundamental values of the past also affected the traditional interpretation of sickness in some points. Thus Deuteronomy 7:12 ff explains the confession transmitted in Exodus 15:22 ff from the perspective of covenant theology and includes sickness in the conditional schema of blessing-curse alternatives that determines the fate of the individual just as it once did the people's. Little is known about the conflicts lying, for example, behind the leprosy section in Deuteronomy 24:8 f, or behind the prescriptions concerning integrity in Deuteronomy 23:2; and above all, little is known about the practice of the commandment of exclusiveness within daily life during the period of kings. In general we know only what is illuminated within the context of prophetic criticism.

4. Structure and Criticism of the Paradigm

We can assume that the still recognizable fixing and formation of the behavioral paradigm for a sick person occurred during the postexilic period. The psalm texts, which to some extent can be dated and which are determinative, lead us to this conclusion (e.g. Ps. 107). In its fully developed form it is then documented at a relatively late date in Job 33. The role paradigm determines the focus and behavior of the individual sick person, as shown by a series of psalm texts as well as by the advice contained in the friends' speeches in the Book of Job. "Behold, God does all these things, twice, three times, with a man" (33:29). The postexilic period also shows us the beginnings of the struggle with that role paradigm in the form of the question asking whether the fundamental ethical law within the present behavior–subsequent fate context (sickness is [God's] punishment, and its reversal: whoever is sick must have sinned), can be maintained in the face of life's realities. Psalm 73 works its way once more to an acknowledgment, admittedly by including the future element (itself including the realm beyond the grave) as the great possibility of equalization. The poet of the Book of Job mounts a serious attack on the paradigm and its basic law by showing that there are cases originating, as it were, in heaven, that do not fit into the paradigm "sickness as God's test or experiment." In view of the addition of the Elihu speeches (Job 33) to the dialogue poetry, we must doubt whether this poetry's explosive power was strong enough to loosen the securely fastened cultic-ethical practices, or even to undo them. In any case, a critical element is brought into the dominant illness ideology through Job with an explosive force that in the Old Testament never had its full effect.

5. The Conflict with Medicine and Exorcism

Under Hellenistic influence, the dispute with the expanding art of medicine was forced on the Yahweh faith, a faith long fixed dogmatically in the question concerning sickness. This dispute was previously carried on in ancient Israel only in the form of critique and polemic against all kinds of subreligious healing practices mixed with charms and magic; cultic law and prophecy worked together here (e.g., in Deut. 18 and Ezek. 13). The dispute had to be taken up again and continued on a higher level during the expansion to a more rational healing art based on diagnosis and therapy, and an expansion also based on the standing of physicians in Israel. Although the narratives in Chronicles were still composed from a conservative perspective in the sense of an either-or, Jesus Sirach shows us a completely different picture. Physicians and the art of healing seem almost effortlessly integrated into the Yahweh faith. Only the theological objection in Sirach 37 f suggests that this was previously a hotly contested area now lying open.

On the other side as well, an easing of the previously unyielding, rigorous position appears to have made an entrance. In any case, the Tobit narrative permits pious Jews to employ exorcism practices too, if they prove to be of divine origin. Here too, sickness appears to gradually become more and more a concern of mediating authorities, even if never completely removed from the divine realm of authority; this is true not only of the immediate causes, but also of the treatment. In ancient Israel as well, we increasingly find demons and angels, exorcists and physicians surrounding the sick person's bed, a person who understands himself to be subject to their powers.

6. Open Questions on the Periphery of the Old Testament

1. The social situation of the sick person in Old Testament times was lamentable. What is known from narratives and psalms

concerning this suggests that considerable human distress existed, resulting largely from the attitude of the culture toward the sick person. This attitude was in its own turn influenced by the reigning religious ideology with its iron-clad law of behavior-consequence. Whoever is sick is himself to blame for it. The obvious absence of any sort of institution providing for the care of the sick, or for the care of the family should its means of support be lost, is particularly noticeable if one compares the legal system in ancient Israel, so much better organized and functioning; this absence can probably be traced back, at least in part, to this basic attitude. The case of the so-called leper was particularly serious. Cultic purity laws, old customs, and elements of a sacral medicine all combined in a role image that had terrible consequences. Arbitrariness in the selection and transmission of Torah texts gave this case a weight that, in comparison to other sicknesses, could not be attributed to it even in the sense of the law, and the longer this arbitrariness was effective, the greater was that weight. Did solidarity commandments such as Leviticus 19:18, insights of later wisdom (Job), or, in general, the communally bound and obligated Yahweh faith simply not ever get under way, or did this faith ultimately stand in its own way in the form of the theodicy dogma?

2. The medicinal store of knowledge in ancient Israel was, to all appearances, minimal, and was first historically and geographically, then religiously, determined. The art of medicine was apparently not even able to establish itself in royal circles in Israel (as it had done in Egypt and in the Fertile Crescent). To the very last, medicine appeared to the Yahweh faith as a heathen art bound in an alien religious fashion, mixed with incantations and magic, an art whose ambiguous practices it could only reject—with the exception of a few techniques of treating wounds. Perhaps all this looked totally different in daily life. The official theology, however, all the way into the Hellenistic period, was not able to develop a positive relationship with medicine (cf., however, Sir. 38). Would this have been possible if ancient Israel had known something besides merely the activities of the soothsayers and magicians, belief in demons, and defense mechanisms such as incantations

and amulets? If it had also known something of that medicinal knowledge and competence brought to light by the Egyptian medicinal papyri and the cuneiform inscriptions?

3. Only cultic institutions offered actual aid to the sick person in ancient Israel. This included the penitential and lament ritual, the visit of the priest (Job 33), the rehabilitating thanksgiving and atonement ritual at the sanctuary—known from the traditions of the Zion sanctuary in Jerusalm—and finally, the behavioral paradigm taken up and reflected upon by Wisdom. What if, however, the institutional bases or even the theological presuppositions for all this were no longer given? What if the paradigm were no longer the generally recognized possession of all those belonging to the Yahweh faith? Many psalms (39; 73) suggest, as does Job, that the self-evident character of this was lost, a self-evidence on which, for example, Job's friends and Psalm 32 still figure. How should the sick person conduct himself in that case?

4. All "theology of sickness" in ancient Israel proceeded on the basis of the *solus* Yahweh, and saw Yahweh's providence in the situation of the sick person, willed by Yahweh, decided, and effected, and all this on the basis of a behavioral norm defined in various ways. Outside the guilt-punishment equation, this norm could also be characterized by intentions directed at pedagogy, testing, or purification. The immediacy of the intercession and the direct dependency was more complemented than relativized by the few instrumentally employed authorities (the sickness demon, Ps. 91:5 f; Satan, Job 1; Yahweh's word, Ps. 107:20). However, it appears this directness was increasingly more difficult to maintain in the later postexilic period. This, however, calls the entire previously valid interpretation of sickness into question. Was it able to assert itself in changed conditions, in other forms of life, among other views of life and other societal conditions?

B.
NEW TESTAMENT

I. Sickness and Healing in the New Testament Milieu

1. The Greek Sphere

During the age of Western antiquity, man attempted to deal in various ways with sickness as an immediate threat to human existence. In this context we can distinguish four institutions available to sick people who wanted to rid themselves of their afflictions.

a) We first ought to mention the *physicians,* who practiced their art in the context of an *empirically* based medicine. If we look at the famous Hippocratic oath,[1] which formulates certain ethical obligations for the physician, we find a three-part separation of physicians' methods of treatment.

> I will employ dietetic measures for the advantage of the sick according to my ability and judgement. . . .
> I will neither give anyone a fatal medicine. . . .
> Neither will I use the knife for those suffering from stone [or to translate: I will not use the knife, not even on those suffering from stone] but will rather abstain from that for the sake of the men who deal in this work.

According to the information in the oath, medicine is basically subdivided into diet, pharmacology, and surgery. However, from the third obligation we can see that operative surgery is to be omitted from the physician's activity. This is not the general view of Greek medicine, but is rather a result of the influence of the Pythagorean physicians' school—which did not value surgery very highly—or of popular prejudice. In antiquity there was a strong prejudice, specifically among the common people, against "cutting and burning." The stone-cut mentioned in the oath was otherwise an old and established procedure in Greek medicine. The diagnosis of the sickness at hand with the help of a catheter was part of the art of a good physician.[2] This example also clearly shows us the empirically based nature of Greek medicine, which sought to explain the causes of sickness by means of concrete examination of the body.

The hostility of many Hippocratic writings toward magic becomes particularly visible. The Hippocratic author of the writing on the "holy sickness" (epilepsy) argues that "all sicknesses, including the holy sickness, are natural and that there is no room for magic as regards cause and treatment."[3]

In Plato we find a differentiation among physicians; this signals the existence of a hierarchy and affected Greek medicine long afterward. It states, basically, as Galen also said later, that the best physician would also have to be a philosopher. Plato first names physicians who treated the afflictions of free men in such a way "that they examine them from the very beginning according to the course of nature." In addition there are others, "whether free born or slaves, who have acquired their art under the tutelage of their masters, by means of observation and practice, and not by means of a study of nature." (*Laws* IV 720). One kind of physician pursues a study following nature, the other acquires the system by means of simple practice with the former. Plato is probably thinking of a practitioner when he writes (*Republic* III 15 406 D): "If a carpenter is sick, he expects his physician to give him medicine which acts as an emetic against the illness, or he expects to be rid of it by means of purging, burning out, or by means of the knife." The practitioner may know a great deal here, but his knowledge is limited to an acquaintance with procedures. The true physician knows the theory that first explains the procedures. He can give reasons for his actions. Just as one can only know the nature of the soul by knowing the nature of the whole, so also can one know the nature of the body only by understanding the whole, the surrounding world of nature (*Phaidros* 270 C). According to Hippocratic medicine, empiricism and natural-philosophical speculation must emerge. The person versed in healing will perfect his craft only if "he makes an effort to gain an insight into the essence of the macrocosm and microcosm and into the causal nexus of functional disturbances by means of (natural-philosophical) reflection and untiring empirical research in nature and at the sickbed."[4] Correspondingly, Plato can then say: not every person is a physician who is able to have an effect on the body by means of his procedures so that it becomes hot or cold at will, or who can cause vomiting or diarrhea or something similar; such a person only knows the prerequisites for the art of healing, but not the art of healing itself (*Phaidros* 268 AB and 269 A). Medicine should rather strive for a knowledge of what is highest, and for that, the true physician must be a philosopher.

This is not the place to go into the natural-philosophical leanings of the various schools of physicians. Nonetheless, an essential characteristic of Greek medicine becomes visible: the association of empirical inquiry with a natural-philosophical interpretation of individual phenomena within the framework of a total view of the cosmos. We find nothing corresponding to these two characteristics in the early Christian view of sickness. This is not surprising at all. In its own way, Greek medicine claimed to be a genuine science. In the New Testament statements, however, we find ourselves in the realm of folk medicine; for example, when the author of 1 Timothy offers the well-intentioned advice (5:23): "No longer drink only water, but use a little wine for the sake of your stomach and your frequent ailments."

For the rest, the dominant view in the New Testament is that demons are the causes of sickness, not naturally occurring, unfavorable bodily developments; this is the difference between this view and all scientific views of sickness. In Greece, too, there was always a "superstitious" interpretation of illness. Plato's *Laws* (932e-933e) and the Attic curse tablets from the fifth/fourth century B.C. witness to its existence in classical Greece. Treatment of illness with the help of magical practices continued to live in the underground. During the period of the Roman empires of the Caesar's, the empirical science of medicine retreated in favor of an increasing irrationalism. Religious medicine stepped to the fore.[5]

b) After the healing activities of physicans, we need to mention the *cultic healing places;* among these, special attention should be given the locale of the god Aesculapius in Epidaurus (since the sixth century B.C.). Filial branches of this god could

also be found in Sikyon, Athens (in the year 420 B.C.) and
Pergamon. Other gods of healing were Isis and Serapis, who had
their various cultic places. In the following presentation we will
use, as our point of orientation, the reports of "Healings of Apollo
and Aesculapius" which once were written on stone plates and
were read with astonishment by pious visitors to the sanctuary. [6]
When Pausanias read them in A.D. 165, they were already quite
old (written approximately in the second half of the fourth
century B.C.). He reports accordingly: "In earlier times even
more inscriptions stood within the boundary (of the sanctuary),
though during my time only six were left. On them were written
the names of men and women whom Aesculapius had healed, as
well as the sickness each of them had and how he was healed"
(*Description of Greece* II 27:3). These places of healing were
there for all social levels, even though the poor sought them out
more than others because they were not able to afford expensive
physicians. One can quickly find a fundamental line of
demarcation between the healing activity of physicians and
healings in the sanctuary: "Because the help of human physicians
had failed, the sick came to the god for whom the impossible is
possible." [7] Therapy was not at all supposed to proceed according
to the art of mortal physicians, but rather through the god. [8]
People sought out the sanctuary in order to experience the god's
powers through the temple sleep (incubation). The god appeared
in a dream to the person seeking healing, gave him specific
instructions or healed him by means of direct intercession
experienced by the sick person in the dream. Thus Aesculapius
provided aid for difficult pregnancies, festering and running
sores, wounds, eye afflictions, speech impediments, paralysis
and illnesses which could only be mastered by an operative
intercession. Aesculapius allegedly also undertook operations
that contemporary medicine did not yet risk, "with wise
knowledge of their limits, insufficient anatomical knowledge,
and faulty hygienic conditions." [9] Thus, in certain cases, "the
stomach was cut open and sewed together again after the removal
of the parasites" (*Miracles* Nr. 23, 25, 27). Praxagoras in Kos was
the first who actually risked opening the stomach cavity (in the
last decades of the fourth century B.C.). Erasistratos in Alexandria

reports similar activities (first half of the third century B.C.), but the fantastic reports from Epidaurus are probably to be interpreted from the perspective of dream psychology.[10] The sick person only dreamed the extraordinary operations. Fantasy has here preceded reality precisely because the god performed cures that, in and for themselves, were considered "impossible or improbable." In spite of characteristics of magic in the healing rituals, the practices in the cultic healing places cannot be completely separated from the physicians' activities. The physician Galen, who came from Pergamon, proudly calls himself the "therapist of his paternal god Aesculapius," who rescued him from a deadly disease. In the Asclepieion in Kos, physicians also had a part, participated in the activities and took care of the sick.[11] Religion and archaic medicine are united in the views concerning the god's healing. The god "acted as a physician; his healings were miracles—for his success was beyond all human reach—but they were strictly medical miracles. On the other hand, this rationality of Aesculapius' treatment seems strangely interwoven with the fantastic and the unreal."[12] In the healing reports from Epidaurus, one encounters sickness as a primally experienced threat to man that can be changed, in the final analysis, only by the god's mercy (*Miracles,* Nr. 1). When Eratocles of Trozen was suffering from a boil and was about to "have himself burned by the physicians, the god appeared to him in sleep and ordered him *not* to have the burning done, but rather to sleep in the healing room in the sanctuary at Epidaurus" (*Miracles,* Nr. 48). Sickness is here a quantity, within the framework of popular-magical thinking, that cannot simply be healed by means of empirical diagnosis and therapy; it needs rather the miraculous power of the god.

c) The *art of magic* was a means of treating sickness that was much in demand. It was not officially allowed, was forbidden by the state, and thus took place in secret. In times of societal disintegration, particularly among the lower social classes, magic offered a means of coming to terms with the problems of life. One characteristic is its "technical optimism": "Under the conditions of that time, in a demoralized world . . . magic represented . . . an optimistic current. While the adherents of the traditional beliefs foresee the collapse of the world in which they live, the magicians believe in the power of the word and of the ritual upon which the old world was based, and they know how to create new rituals adapted to the new needs and founded upon a new understanding of man."[13] The sequence of the magic activity had to be precisely controlled so that the ritual could unfold its effect. The magical act was thus often divided into four parts: the conjuring of the demon, consisting of a magic incantation or prayer; the sacrifice; the actual magical act itself, in which specific magical practices were performed; and the release of the demon. Magic also included the word, or the magical formula, by means of which the demon was to be coerced so that it obeyed the will of the magician. One acquired this power over the demon through knowledge of its name, which one then spoke out loud in order to bring the demon into service. The power of magic words was considered particularly strong if they contained "barbaric names," i.e., foreign words. Finally, magic words were to be spoken softly or in secret so that no other person could hear them.

Exorcism healings also belonged in the realm of magic, and were employed against sicknesses considered particularly serious or dangerous, against forms of possession such as epilepsy and other mental illnesses. Thus we read, for example, some instructions to an exorcist (PGM XIII 242-44)[14]: "Speak to a demonically possessed person the name and bring sulphur and resin to his nose. He will immediately speak and will go away." Within an entire magic procedure, an incantation of the demon dominating the sick person sounds as follows (PGM IV 1240 ff): "I adjure you, demon, whoever you may be, in the name of this god . . . come out, demon, whoever you may be and remove yourself from N. N., now, now, immediately, immediately." For magic, the world is ruled by dark powers, and sickness seems to be the result of demonic activity. At the same time, however, the conjurer is certain of being able to oppose this threat successfully by knowing efficacious words and materials.

d) *Miracle charismatics* need to be distinguished from magicians. While the magician carries on his practices in secret, the miracle charismatic solicits "in open public, precipitates missionary movements or founds 'schools,'—not because he wants to be integrated into the existing form of life (here lies the difference with the function of healing places)—but rather because he is seeking new forms of life which can be socially relevant."[15] The miracles announced by the messianic prophets in Palestine during the first century of the Christian era were thus supposed to demonstrate the advent of the time of salvation and the end of Roman rule. The miraculous healings of Apollonius of Tyana are extensively significant in another way. They took place within the context of his philosophical-religious doctrine of healing. Philostratus, who wrote a *vita* of Apollonius, places him, with some justification, together with the philosophers Pythagoras and Empedocles, the latter having functioned in particular as a miracle worker (*Diogenes Laertius* VIII 61): "He saved from Persephone's arm many who were pursued by fate and afflicted by wasting sickness."

The figure of the Emperor Vespasian also takes on characteristics of such charismatics, and he uses the legitimizing function of miracles for political purposes. In any case, miracles stand in the service of a specific program. The report of his healings begins with the words: "Vespasian still lacked the necessary reputation and as it were the majesty confirmed by god, since he was only recently elevated to Caesar against all expectation. But this, too, he acquired" (Suetonius, *Vespasian* 7). There then follows the description of the healing of a blind person and a cripple.

In spite of the difference between magicians and miracle charismatics, which was totally in keeping with their own self-understanding, the charge of magic was often raised against the charismatics. Apollonius, for example, is accused of being a magician. As regards the extra-Jewish arena in Hellenism, this is also understandable. Their own miraculous healing practices are not always that much different from those of magic, for example, the use of miraculously effective words that had to be spoken as silently as possible. Thus Apollonius speaks the decisive words secretly (Philostratus, *Life of Apollonius* IV 45, compare also the magicians in Lucian, *Menippus* 7).

Within the Greek realm the activity of miracle men was viewed as being "divine," since they possessed knowledge and competency equal to that of the gods *(Life of Apollonius* III 42). One sees a contrast to the activities of physicians, for example, in the attitude of the public towards them. Just as one sought help from the healing god if the physicians failed, so also did one do this in the case of the miracle worker. His ability exceeded that of the physicians. Philostratus thus makes the following remark in view of the resurrection from the dead of a girl by Apollonius *(Life of Apollonius* IV 45): "Words were not enough to enable either me or those present to comprehend whether he found a spark of life in her which had remained hidden to the *physicians* . . . or whether he rekindled and recalled the extinguished life." We hear about Empedocles: "He healed a certain Pantheia from Akrygos, who had been given up by the physicians . . . " *(Diogenes Laertius* VIII 69)

2. The Jewish Sphere

Judaism during the New Testament period belongs in the wide realm of ancient Hellenism. It is a many-layered quantity which sought its identity either in the assumption or the rejection of Greek-Hellenistic ideas. Even when trying to differentiate itself from Hellenism (e.g., as did the "pious" during the Maccabean period or the zealots during Jesus' time), the "genuine" Jewish position—building on the old traditions of Israel—is only comprehensible as a reaction to the simultaneous Hellenizing tendencies of opposing circles.

The Israelite idea of "Yahweh's healing monopoly" (cf. Part I, "Old Testament" [OT] II.5; IV.2) had a powerful, lasting effect in Judaism. Sickness itself, and particularly its healing, is Yahweh's exclusive work. This view had no other parallels in Hellenism. Though Aesculapius might be a healing god, praised by his worshipers with glowing words, he nonetheless tolerated having Apollo, from whom he had inherited his functions, right next to him in the inscription of Epidaurus or in the Hippocratic oath.

Skepticism and even the rejection of physicians' treatments are connected with "Yahweh's healing monopoly" in Judaism (OT I.4; IV.5). This did indeed have its parallels in Hellenistic miracle reports. It is practically a hallmark of the miracle-healing genre to speak of the failure of the physicians in order to let the healing god's power shine all the more brightly. Skepticism toward the physicians, however, is based here primarily on their practical failures, and is not religiously motivated. This skepticism is, however, religiously motivated within pious Judaism.

Even the Jewish philosopher Philo of Alexandria, who lived in the hotbed of ancient medicine at that time and was strongly influenced by Greek thought, is critical of physicians' help and the trust many people put in those physicians. He says the following about those who doubt God's effectiveness:

> For whenever something unpleasant happens, they take—because they previously did not trust in the help of God—they take refuge in the earthly aids, physicians, herbs, medicine mixtures, exact diets and all the other measures standing at the disposal of the mortal beings. And if one should perhaps say: "You fools, flee to the only physician of spiritual maladies and let go of the husk falsely named by mankind which is capable of suffering," then they laugh and mock and cry: "That tomorrow!" (*Concerning the Sacrifice of Abel and Cain* 70).

God appears here in the true Old Testment manner as "the only physician"; physicians and medicines are only a means of help for mortals.

We find something similar in a writing also composed within Greek-speaking Judaism: Testament Job 38. The friends of the sick Job ask him:

> What do you want us to do for you? For behold, we are there, and with us the physicians from our three kingdoms. Do you want to let yourself be healed by them?

Job, however, answers:

> My healing and my recovery are from the Lord, who also created the physicians.

The skeptical, sometimes rigidly rejecting attitude toward physicians did not change in the Judaism of the Talmudic period:

> The best among the physicians deserves Gehenna, and the most noble among the butchers is a companion of Amalek. (b Kidd.82a)

> Rabh spoke to his son Chiya: "Do not drink medicines. Do not jump across rivers. Do not let anyone pull your teeth. Do not irritate any snake nor any Aramaean." (b Pes. 113a)

In another passage the seeking of the physician is indeed permitted, but the physican's treatment should be subordinated to God's activity by means of a prayer (b Ber. 60a):

> Whoever goes to have his blood let, let him speak: May it be your will, O Lord my God, that this treatment serve my recovery and heal me, for you, O God, are the true physician, and your healing is real.

In another way, a healing is justified religiously in the Book of Tobit (around 200 B.C.) which owes its origin to folk medicine, which itself is influenced by magic views (OT II.1). This particular manner of healing is only possible because the angel of God himself, Raphael, conveys the particular healing method (6:8 f) and finally gives the instructions for the healing (11:6-12). "Yahweh's healing monopoly" is thus preserved.

Similarly, a mantic-magical kind of medicine appears to have been theologically based among the Essenes. Josephus writes the following about this special group within Judaism (*Jewish Wars* 2, 136): "However, they go to a great deal of effort concerning the writings of the ancients; in this they choose that which advances soul and body. From these writings they research medicinal roots and the [occult] characteristics of stones for the purpose of healing sicknesses."

The Essenes' art of healing here, based on old writings, acquires more definite contours if one studies the apocryphal book of Jubilees, fragments of which were found in the Essenes' library in Qumran. We find that sicknesses had demonic origins

and could only be healed by magical means. In order to treat
them successfully, a kind of opposing magic was thus necessary;
its administration was mediated to selected persons by God's
angels and thus could be considered legitimate. These angels
revealed to Noah the healing of all sicknesses, "so that he might
heal through the earth's trees [plants]." And Noah wrote down all
they had taught him "in a book, about all manners of healing"
(Jubilees 10:12 ff). "Roots," "plants," and the "properties of
stones" were considered to be magically effective means of
healing in antiquity. Just how one is to imagine this concretely
can be seen from a report by Josephus concerning King
Solomon's healing ability, which even during Josephus' time was
still believed within Judaism (*Jewish Antiquities* VIII 2, 5), as
Josephus expressly emphasizes:

> God also taught him [Solomon] the art of banning evil spirits
> for the advantage and good of men. He composed namely
> sayings concerning the healing of sicknesses and incantation
> formulas, with which one can thus bind and drive out the
> spirits, so that they never again return. *This art of healing is
> still valid with us today.*

Josephus also claims to have seen himself how a Jew by the name
of Eleazar healed a possessed person in the presence of the
emperor Vespasian and his retinue (*Jewish Antiquities* VIII 2, 5):
"He held a ring under the nose of the possessed person in which
one of the roots was enclosed which Solomon had suggested; he
let the sick person smell it and in that way pulled the evil spirit
out through the nose."

    The Jewish healing arts, to the extent they were considered
legitimate, differentiated themselves in a fundamental way from
the more rational methods which were characteristic of empirical
medicine at that time, a medicine having its main center in
Hellenistic Alexandria. The physicians' activities were strongly
permeated by magical practices they justified by tracing
knowledge of them back to God's angels or to Solomon. Demons
and evil spirits were considered to be the cause or authors of
sicknesses, which accordingly would only be combatted by a

commensurate "white anti-magic." This demonological under-standing was able to establish and maintain itself in Judaism because a scientific examination of the human body and anatomy was impossible for religious reasons. Knowledge of the anatomical structure of the body as well as of its physiological processes was accordingly extremely limited.

In addition to magic and magically operating healing arts, which Josephus openly says were highly considered by Jews, there are also indications of an empirically working medicine, traceable, however, back to the influence of the Greek surroundings. The most significant documentation is found in the book of Jesus Sirach in the so-called "Praise of the Physician" (Sir. 38:1-15). Although the author generally follows an anti-Hellenistic inclination in order to defend the faith of the fathers, he is nonetheless influenced by the opposing position. Thus it is not surprising that his opinion of the activity of the physician ends up being self-contradictory. One sees initially that he skeptically condemns medical arts:

A long illness baffles the physician; the king of today will die tomorrow. . . . (Sir. 10:10)

He who sins before his Maker, may he fall into the care of a physician. (Sir. 38:15)

What follows, however, is more important. Jesus Sirach stands before the theological problem of solving the discrepancy between the divine and medical activities. For him, too, the Old Testament conviction concerning "Yahweh's healing monopoly" holds true; at the same time, however, he maintains the rational insight into the necessity of the physician. He attempts to transcend this contradiction by understanding the physician as a creation of God and as his tool (38:1-5)[16]:

Honor the physician with the honor due him, according to your need of him, for the Lord created him; for healing comes from the Most High . . . The Lord created medicines from the earth, and a sensible man will not despise them . . . And he gave skill to men . . . By them he heals and takes away pain;

the pharmacist makes of them a compound. His works will never be finished; and from him health is upon the face of the earth.

My son, when you are sick do not be negligent, but pray to the Lord, and he will heal you . . . And give the physician his place, for the Lord created him; let him not leave you, for there is need of him. There is a time when success lies in the hands of physicians, for they too will pray to the Lord that he should grant them success in diagnosis and in healing, for the sake of preserving life.

It is significant that this text does not view sickness demonologically. Sickness is not traced back to the damaging activity of demons or evil spirits, as is otherwise the case in Judaism. We already see a rational inclination here allowing us to conclude that the kind of medicine meant here is empirically directed and presupposes a natural explanation of sickness. The medicines, probably made of plants, come from the earth. With them the physician removes pain and from them the pharmacist prepares his mixture. This description also suggests that the entire healing procedure does without magical practices and is based on the natural effect of, for example, healing herbs.

This rational view of sickness and healing was possible because of the creation faith that characterizes the entire text. Just as in the priestly account of creation (Gen. 1), all occurrences in nature have been robbed of their divine or demonic character and have become creations of God, lacking any magically effective independence. Here too: God causes healing substances to grow from the earth which bring about healing because of their (no longer magical) effective properties. The creation faith removed the demonic character of the world and all things existing in it, thus freeing man's vision for a natural view of the world, which in its own turn made empirical medicine possible. The creation faith, emphasized in this way, was the prerequisite for a borrowing of medical ideas as they were practiced in part in Hellenistic medicine.

Jesus Sirach stands rather isolated in this posture within the pious Judaism of his time. For the rest, we hear very little about the activity of empirically working physicians. An understandable exception is the Hellenistically influenced court of the Judaean kings. The mortally ill Herod the Great (died 4 B.C.) had himself treated by physicians who were probably Greek. Josephus gives us a thorough report of his sickness, though it is difficult to give a sure diagnosis in the modern sense—a state of affairs that will occur in increasing measure in the New Testament descriptions of sickness. Josephus' text, *Jewish Antiquities* XVII 6, 5, reads as follows:

> The fever was weak and when touched did not show the inflammation to be as large as the devastation caused inside. There developed a fearful urge to scratch incessantly on some place, for there was no possibility of employing any aid; further, there was a swelling of the innards and particularly bad pains in the intestines and a moist, shiny, slimy inflammation of the feet. A similar malady was also in the stomach, probably also decay on the genitals, caused by worms.[17]

The physicians prescribed warm baths in the fountains of Kallirhoë, which flows in to the Dead Sea. When that did not help, Herod had to bathe his entire body in warm oil—a procedure that almost killed him. Herod finally died from his illness.

Josephus' report shows us in an exemplary fashion what kind of healing cures rich and powerful people in Palestine were able to use. They correspond to those otherwise customary in Hellenistic healing baths as well. The medicinal activity, as it was open to rich people in Kallirhoë or similar places, was condemned from the perspective of poorer Jews: "Those waters, however, will in those days serve the healing of the bodies and the punishment of the spirit for the kings, powerful and high ones who live on the firm land, because their spirit is full of debauchery so that their bodies are punished" (Book of Enoch 67:8). This polemic directs itself against the sinfulness of those "powerful and high persons" who will not find healing in their cures, but rather will suffer punishment. However, behind these attacks there may also stand a mistrust of Hellenistic healing

activities as such which could not be brought into harmony with
the old patriarchal faith.

If one surveys the view of sickness within Judaism, four
kinds of explanation can be ascertained.

a) In the Wisdom literature, particularly in the book Jesus
Sirach, we find a rational view of sickness. Accordingly,
physicians employ healing substances that have a natural effect,
not a magical one (Sir. 38:1-15). Sickness has natural causes.
Excessive eating causes sleeplessness and vomiting (Sir. 31 [34]:
20 ff). Every excess calls forth afflictions (37:27 ff). This
rationality is made possible by the emphatic faith in God as
creator who knows no other powers (Sir. 39:16, 33). This basic
view, however, was not able to establish itself in Judaism. To be
sure, rabbinic Judaism does value plant healing substances such
as oil and wine. But this trafficking with methods of folk
medicine, which includes the belief in a natural effect of such
substances, was not able to prevent the spread of the
demonological understanding of sickness. The procedures of folk
medicine did indeed come from the everyday experiential world;
but the life of concrete experience, which always renders at least
a modicum of rationality possible, was nonetheless powerless in
the face of the growing belief in demons (cf. OT IV.5).

b) Just as do many circles throughout antiquity, so also does
Judaism believe that sickness can be traced back to the effect of
demons. We can here presume that the belief in demons
gradually increased. In the Old Testament there is only
peripheral talk of a demonological view of sickness (e.g. Ps. 91:6).
Things are different in the postbiblical writings of Judaism.
Jubilees 10:10, 12 f speaks at great length about this: "He [God]
said to one of us [angels]: We want to teach Noah all their
healings [i.e., the healing of sickness caused by demons]. . . .
And we told Noah all the healings of their sickness including the
knowledge of their procedures so that he might heal by means of
the trees of the earth."

The Greek Book of Baruch 16:3 deals, in general, with
sickness demons, and in the writing, "Life of the Prophets" 16,
King Nebuchadnezzar is attacked by a demon who causes his
madness. In the rabbinic writings these views are virtually

systematized. Quite specific spirits are assigned to the individual sickness they are thought to cause. There is the spirit of perplexity or of delirium, the spirit of catalepsy or of stupor, the spirit of asthma or of heart trouble, and so on.[18] Blindness is occasionally traced back to the demon Shabriri.[19] Epilepsy, or even lameness, dumbness, deafness, and blindness of children can have their bases in the parents' improper behavior during sexual intercourse, since the time of sexual intercourse was considered to be threatened by demons.[20]

c) For ancient Israel, weakness, sickness, captivity and other threats belong to the domain of death (cf. OT II.2). Whoever is so sick that he is limited in his life possibilities— death is exerting its power over that person. He is like a dead person, since he has come into contact with the reality of death. This kind of thinking appears to have experienced a certain continuation in Judaism. Thus one often hears: "Four are considered the equal of a dead person: the poor, the leprous, the blind, and the childless" (e.g. b Ned. 64 b). Or: Elisha "healed Naaman's leprosy, who was considered equal with death" (b Sanh. 47 a). To be sure, this view did not have the same significance for later Judaism as it did in ancient Israel.

d) Rabbinic Judaism claims a close connection between sin and sickness as the consequent punishment. It systematically worked out this conception and developed it in detail. God sees to it that guilt and punishment are related according to the principle "measure for measure."[21] Appropriate transgressions were suggested for many illnesses. Incontinence was the reason for a certain kind of dropsy that causes the body to be hard, and in a case of magic the body becomes wasted (b Shabb. 33a Bar.). Quinsy arises because of neglected fruit tithes or because of slander (b Shabb. 33a Bar.). Conversely, one knew the resulting punishment for every transgression of the law. Whoever engages in sexual intercourse under the light of a lamp will have epileptic children (Pes. 112 b Bar.). Leprosy plagues come upon man because of eleven things: idolatry, profanation of the divine name, incontinence, thievery, slander, and so on.[22]

Because of the connection between sin and sickness, healing must be preceded by the forgiveness of sins. Rabbi Alexandrai (around 270) thus says: "The sick person will not arise from his sickness until one [i.e., God] has forgiven him all his sins, behold: 'Who forgives all your iniquity, who heals all your diseases' " (Psalm 103:3 [b Ned. 41 a]).[23] Thus prayer or even a guilt sacrifice and oath are necessary to reconcile God's wrath. The greatest miracle worker of rabbinic Judaism, Rabbi Chanina ben Dosa (second half of the first century of the Christian Era), healed only by means of prayer, and not through magical practices (b Berakh 34 b)[24]:

> The son of Rabbi Gamaliel once became sick [Gamaliel II around A.D. 90). He sent two learned pupils to Rabbi Chanina ben Dosa to request that he might pray for mercy for him. When he saw these two, he went up to the balcony and prayed for mercy for him. When he came back down he said to them: Go, for the fever has left him. They spoke to him: Are you perhaps a prophet? He answerd them: I am no prophet, and not the son of a prophet, but thus have I received it . . .: When my prayer is easy in my mouth (when it passes my lips without faltering) then I know that the person concerned is accepted.

II. Jesus'
Understanding of
Sickness and Healing

1. Methods, Preliminary Considerations

Before we can deal with Jesus' understanding of sickness and healing, some preliminary methodological clarification is necessary. One cannot avoid determining the circle of textual statements that can, with some degree of certainty, be attributed to Jesus. If one looks at the gospels, at first glance there seems to be first-rate source material in the healing stories there, since in

them Jesus is clearly confronted with the phenomenon of
sickness. However, critical scholarship has concluded with
relative certainty that all the Jesus *stories* have been influenced
in large measure by the faith and views of the post-Easter
community, so that they do not simply give us the views of the
historical Jesus in a direct fashion. This is not surprising at all. All
the Jesus stories, and therefore also the healing accounts, were
narrated by Christians of the post-Easter community. These
narrators naturally let their own thoughts and problems flow into
the stories quite unconsciously. The longer and more complicated this process of tradition has gone on, the more difficult does
it become to separate a possible historical core, which would lead
to the earthly Jesus, from the influences of post-Easter shaping.
One of Jesus' healings, related before Easter by the first
disciples, has thus undergone manifold changes up to the oldest
literary stage in which it is accessible to us (in the gospel of Mark
about A.D. 70). Let us explain this more precisely as regards
certain points. A comprehensive comparison of Jewish, Gentile-
Hellenistic, and Christian miracle stories shows that these
stories, and thus also accounts of Jesus' healings, were formed
according to certain recurring narrative schemata. This was not
done consciously or intentionally. There was, rather, a
widespread custom of telling healing stories in this and no other
way; playing a role here is the fact that people interpreted
healings of sick people with the very old traditional interpreta-
tive categories of a transmitted belief in miracles. Thus the
modern reader of Jesus' miracle stories becomes acquainted first
and foremost with the thought horizon of those early Christian
narrators, and only in a quite limited fashion with that of the main
actor in these stories, namely Jesus. This problem is additionally
aggravated by the fact that the original accounts of Jesus' healings
stimulated the fantasy of those post-Easter narrators in such a
way that new stories were "invented." Therefore, these are not
historical in the sense that they offer information about the
historical Jesus, but rather information about the faith of early
Christians. The formation of new miracle stories was provoked in
a particular way within the competitive situation of the early
Christian mission. People were hearing about the amazing

miraculous healings of heathen gods and miracle workers (such as healings from a distance and resurrections of the dead). Since, however, the narrators were deeply convinced that Jesus was *the* Son of God, of the Most High (cf. Mark 5:7), the Son who surpassed all "sons of gods," indeed, that he was the only Son of God, they were virtually forced to tell new miracle stories about Jesus in order to outdo the competing stories. They questioned the healings of heathen miracle workers: "Never since the world began has it been heard that any one opened the eyes of a man born blind" (John 9:32), and then claimed precisely this for Jesus. The conviction of Jesus' singularity had to induce one to attribute deeds to him that were denied others.

All this suggests that the healing stories about Jesus are not very suitable for uncovering Jesus of Nazareth's own understanding of sickness. Even in the cases in which a miracle account allegedly can be traced back to one of Jesus' historical healings, the reader chiefly learns something about the views of the Christian narrators, since it is these who determined the story's character by their horizon of interests and their own views. This state of affairs is self-evident in the new stories which originated as analogies to other Jesus stories or because of competition with heathen stories after Easter. To a large extent, the accounts of miracle healings do not qualify as sources for Jesus' understanding of sickness. They will, on the other hand, prove to be outstanding testimonies when it is time to examine the post-Easter community concerning its understanding of healing.

Some of Jesus' *words* can be considered as relatively secure sources for Jesus' view of sickness and healing. In a manner different from the stories, in which narrators only report *about* Jesus, there are sayings in the gospels that let Jesus speak directly and immediately.

2. Jesus' Exorcism of Demons in the Inbreaking Kingdom of God

As we know from the first three Gospels, cases of "possession" were a common phenomenon during Jesus' time.

The sick people were thought to be ruled by demons that resided within them and coerced them into self-destructive behavior (cf. Part II, "New Testament" [NT] III. 1). Saving was effected by exorcizing the injurious demon. Jesus was active as an exorcist in the struggle against these "unclean spirits."

The sayings in Luke 10:18, Luke 11:20 (parallel Matt. 12:28), and Mark 3:27 can be considered to be original words of Jesus that are relevant here. [25] Their authenticity manifests itself in the fact that the presence of God's reign is mentioned without use of analogy. The liberation from the "possession" has a direct relation here to the inbreaking kingdom of God, a relation not predetermined in Judaism in this way. It is an element in the struggle for the establishment of eschatological salvation. Liberation is realized already in the present.

In order to clarify Jesus' view, one had best begin with the relationship between Luke 10:18 and Luke 11:20. In Luke 10:18 Jesus' vision proclaims: "I saw Satan fall like lightning from heaven." Satan was pushed out of heaven by God—this is cause for Jesus to be convinced that God finally intends to establish his kingdom in heaven as well as on earth. The present world era of misfortune and suffering is coming to an end, for God in heaven has set about putting an end to Satan, the cause of the misfortune. Jesus considers himself to be God's tool on earth (Luke 11:20): "But if it is by the finger of God that I cast out demons, then the kingdom of God has come upon you." Jesus exorcizes the demons from the possessed person, and in this way liberates him. The conviction obtains here that wherever this happens, God becomes Lord. How is this to be understood? Satan is considered the prince of demons, their Lord whom they obey as accomplices. If, then, one of Satan's bastions of dominance is destroyed by the exorcism of a demon by Jesus, then his sphere of power on earth is diminished. Correspondingly, God's dominion establishes itself, with whose power Jesus drives out the demons. What apocalyptic believers only expected in the future, namely, the end of Satan and his power (Moses' ascension, 10:1), begins already in Jesus' presence. His exorcism of demons, and with it the victorious struggle against Satan on earth, are visible signs of the advent of the eschatological time of salvation in which God alone will reign. The Stronger is on the move in Jesus' activity, the one who has broken into the "strong man's house," Satan's, and "binds the strong man" (Mark 3:27).

Jesus' interpretation of his own demon exorcisms is singular in religious history. If one looks at miracle charismatics of his time, nowhere does one find this global understanding of individual healings. His exorcisms are actually the expression of the comprehensive changing of the entire world; when a possessed person is healed, thus when a demon is cast out, Satan's dominion undergoes a diminution of power which allows God's dominion in the world to become effective so that misfortune and suffering pass away. God's dominion as the intensely expected future is already becoming visible in Jesus' actions. Jesus combines two aspects not otherwise connected in this way: the expectation of a universal future salvation and the individual realization of present miraculous salvation.

According to the words which probably genuinely come from Jesus, the demonological understanding is one of the prerequisites of his exorcisms transmitted by tradition (Luke 11:20, Mark 3:27). "Possession" was, after all, an affliction caused by the demon residing within the sick person. What is new with Jesus is the eschatological horizon in which the phenomenon of "possession" appears. The struggle against it means the advent of God's reign. To be sure, demonology is not really overcome in a rational, enlightened sense, since the demons are not denied in their factual existence. Nonetheless, there is an overcoming of the belief in demons to the extent that Jesus conquers the demons and thus destroys the really threatening power of sickness. Fear and dread of sickness, particularly of possession, lose their power through the end of the demons. The religious fear, inextricably associated with possession, simultaneously recedes with the removal of the physical malady.

Jesus performed demon exorcisms. A medical evaluation of these activities is of course difficult, because the texts only briefly allude to things and are not at all interested in modern questions. When we say today: "Jesus performed healings which astonished his contemporaries. They were primarily a matter of the healing of psychological afflictions," this statement may be fundamentally correct. When one adds above and beyond that that Jesus performed the demon exorcisms with a brief word of command, thus by means of "happenings along the lines of what doctors call 'overpowering therapy,' "[26] then one has already left the realm of that which can be concluded with certainty from the texts. In the case of such an interpretation, one must seek the help of stories reporting Jesus' demon exorcisms (Mark 5:1-20; 9:14-28). Here, indeed, the exorcist's word of power effects the corresponding miracle (Mark 9:25). In the first place, however, this description is attributed to the topos of ancient exorcisms without the conclusion concerning Jesus' actual method of healing being allowed with further qualification. The stories in Mark 5:1 ff and 9:14 ff initially show only how the post-Easter narrators imagined Jesus' demon exorcisms—namely in analogy with other (including heathen) miracle workers; they do not directly lead us to the historical Jesus himself.

3. Jesus' Healings of Sickness

The saying in Matthew 11:5 f (parallel Luke 7:22 f) could now help give more precise information concerning the various sicknesses Jesus healed. According to well supported opinion, this text represents a passage that was initially transmitted by itself and only later expanded by the addition of the scenic framework in 11:2-4: "The blind receive their sight and the lame walk, lepers are cleansed and the deaf hear, and the dead are raised up, and the poor have good news preached to them. And blessed is he who takes no offense at me" (Matt. 11:5 f).

Matthew 11:5 f probably comes from the mouth of the historical Jesus. The passage's first section (v 5) corresponds with his conviction concerning the presently inbreaking kingdom of God bringing the final salvation (cf. Luke 10:23 f). The second section (v 6) reflects the conflicting situation in which Jesus himself stood. His miracles were not an unambiguous verification of his being sent, as his pious opponents' objections prove,

objections implying that he was associated with Beelzebub and
that by the prince of demons, he cast out the demons (Mark 3:22).

People have wanted to understand this text in such a way
that the enumeration of individual miracles was to legitimize
Jesus' prophetic office, since according to Jewish understanding,
miracles represent a verifying sign for eschatological prophecy.
However, this interpretation is controverted by the observation
that the "enumeration" in verse 5 is not formulated with express
reference to Jesus, but is speaking rather in a quite general and
comprehensive fashion about the signs of the new age.
Furthermore, the concluding sentence presupposes that the
miracles do not simply provide direct legitimization, since the
threatening danger of offense is present. The miraculous deeds
here describe the new age, and do not authorize a person.
However, we are then left with the interpretation saying that the
word intends to portray the salvation epoch which has
commenced and that this word employs images of older
prophecy (Isa. 26:19; 29:18 f; 35:5 f; 61:1) without the individual
statements intending to enumerate a precise protocol of Jesus'
deeds that have already occurred. If this interpretation is
correct, then it is no longer inexplicable why the demon
exorcisms so typical for Jesus are missing in this series. They did
not have to be mentioned, since the passage portrays the
eschatological salvation period in traditional colors and is not
intended to be simply a list of deeds performed by Jesus. This
interpretation does not falter on the fact that, on the other hand,
the healing of lepers is mentioned, even though it does not occur
as an element of Isaiah's salvation period prophecy (Isa. 35:8 is
only a vague beginning), and that it is therefore possibly a part of
the basis of historical reality. This passage has a basis in historical
occurrences without, however, portraying them precisely.
Precisely, because it intends more: it wants to proclaim the
salvation period which has already commenced, of which one can
say (Matt. 13:16 f, par. Luke 10:23 f): "But blessed are your eyes,
for they see, and your ears, for they hear." and (Matt. 11:6 par.
Luke 7:23): "And blessed is he who takes no offense at me."

On the basis of this conclusion, the passage in Matthew
11:5 f (par. Luke 7:22 f), in spite of its probable historical basis

as a saying of Jesus, does not prove to be a secure testimony concerning the scope of Jesus' healing activity. Since the passage primarily employs traditional images and does not so much mention actual healings of sickness—the demon exorcisms are missing—the references to blindness, lameness, and deafness do not offer unambiguous circumstantial proof of the healing of these specific sicknesses. On the other hand, it is unthinkable that Jesus paints the inbreaking salvation period in available images that do not correspond in any way to the actual reality of his healings. In the emphatic mention of the salvation proclamation to the poor at the conclusion of the series, a decisive element of his activity is indeed brought forth (cf. Luke 6:20 f). Thus it is certainly possible that Jesus healed illnesses such as "blindness," "lameness," or "deafness." It is difficult to determine just what kind of understanding of sickness Jesus had in these cases; whether here, too, for example, a demonological interpretation is presupposed. These sicknesses, however, need not lie on a completely different level of interpretation than do Jesus' demon exorcisms.

Nonetheless, caution is advised here. It has always been noticed that the healings in Matthew 11:5 f do not include demon exorcisms. To be sure, the passage does not claim to offer a complete enumeration of Jesus' miraculous works: but it remains astonishing that precisely the exorcisms—so characteristic for Jesus—do not show up. Could this state of affairs not also stem from the fact that Jesus' healings mentioned in the passage lie on a level different from that of the exorcisms? Blindness, lameness, deafness, and leprosy are certainly sicknesses of a nature different than that of "possession." In one instance the demonic damage was at any rate thought to be partially something effected by an external source, if something of this sort was at hand at all (cf. NT IV.2). In the case of possession it was total; the demon resided in the sick person (cf. NT III.1). Sicknesses of different natures need correspondingly appropriate healing methods. The former were healed, as the actual miracle stories will show, by means of a transferral of power; forms of possession, however, by means of a demon exorcism. This difference in Matthew 11:5 f could explain why miracle works of Jesus appear separately here;

all have in common the fact that they are not exorcisms. We cannot yet draw any secure conclusions here. However, these considerations ought to prompt us to pursue further the problem of whether Jesus interpreted sicknesses quite differently and accordingly understood his healings theologically in various different ways.

Related to Jesus' actual words are some stories in whose center one of Jesus' sayings stands. The story of the healing of a crippled hand on the Sabbath belongs here (Mark 3:1-6). It deserves special attention here because Jesus' statement in verse 4, according to the prevalent opinion, is authentic, and implies an attitude concerning the situation of the sick person. Above and beyond that, the entire scene portrayed might be based on a memory still alive. This is supported by the fact that Jesus heals here demonstrably on the Sabbath and provokes the conflict with the pious. Precisely these conflicts with the law are characteristic for Jesus' public activity. To be sure, literary critical analysis shows that this narrative, too, contains many schematic elements coming from the topos of miracle stories as well as of dispute dialogues. Nonetheless, Jesus' authentic statement in verse 4, organically integrated into the narrative, already suggests that the entire conflict scene did not just emerge from the imagination of the post-Easter community.

The story's point of departure is the fact that, on the Sabbath, Jesus encounters a man with a withered hand. Jesus' opponents wait to see whether he will heal the sick person on the Sabbath. This scenic preparation is intended to allow Jesus to engage consciously in the conflict already laid out. He seizes the initiative: "And he said to the man who had the withered hand, 'Come here' " (v 3). Jesus' statement in verse 4 is decisive; in the form of a counter-argument, it responds to the opponents' objection in verse 2: "Is it lawful on the sabbath to do good or to do harm, to save life or to kill?"[27] In the final analysis these questions leave the opponents no real choice, since, naturally, the only possible answer is that one is permitted to do good. The second question concretizes the more general initial question with a view to the questionable healing of the sick person. It is a matter of saving, and here that means (according to the Semitic

background of the Greek word) a matter of making this particular
sick person healthy and alive. Correspondingly, killing no doubt
means the failure to perform the deed that itself restores life.
This corresponds to Old Testament views. There is no neutral
zone, only life or death, good or evil. Earthly life is taken so
seriously that when it involves sickness it can no longer be called
life in the full sense of the word. Thus healing, the act that
restores life, is also necessary on the Sabbath. Its omission would
bring the sick person nearer to death because it would leave him
in the power realm of death. Jesus' statement in verse 4 uncovers
a new aspect in Jesus' understanding of sickness. Sickness is
proximity to death. Jesus thus follows the Old Testament
tradition which was also continued in Judaism: "Four are
considered equal to a dead person: the poor, the leprous, the
blind, and the childless" (b Ned. 64 b Bar.).

This understanding of sickness can be concluded from yet
another of Jesus' sayings. In the originally isolated saying which
the evangelist Matthew inserted into the story in Mark 3:1-6 he
found before him (Matt. 12:11 f par. Luke 14:5), Jesus asks (Matt.
12:11 f): "What man of you, if he has one sheep and it falls into a
pit on the sabbath, will not lay hold of it and lift it out? Of how
much more value is a man than a sheep!" This saying is based on
the doctrine that a threat to the life even of an animal suspends
the Sabbath commandment. How much more—Jesus argues—
does this then hold true for man. As regards the problem of
healing the sick on the Sabbath this means that the healing of that
sick person runs parallel to the saving of the life of an animal from
death, since being sick means already being under the control of
death in some way. The sick person as such has fallen into death's
realm of power, not only because sickness possibly brings
death—that would be modern rational thinking—but because,
on the basis of mythical thought, sickness eo ipso belongs to
death's domain. This is quite clear in the example of the man with
the "withered" hand (Mark 3:1-6). Whatever sickness in the
modern sense might lie behind it (muscular atrophy? a form of
paralysis?) it is not such that it could lead to a quick physical
death, and the narrative knows this quite well, since the legal
problem of Jesus' Sabbath transgression arises precisely because

Jesus heals on the Sabbath even though there is no acute mortal danger. Nonetheless, the sick person is given over to death to the extent that the omission of the healing would be "a killing." Jesus, however, felt called to save the sick person, i.e., to strengthen his life or pull him away from the realm of death.

In Mark 3:1-6 (and Matt. 12:11 f) a view of death for Jesus is suggested which has its significance next to the demonological view: sickness as proximity to death. According to the presuppositions of Jewish thought, these are not competing with each other; sickness and death can be traced back to the activity of demons (Book of Jubilees 10:1 f, 10-13). However, a more thorough interpretation is suggesting itself which already outlined a possibility during the discussion of Matthew 11:5 f. If Luke 13:32 is a genuine statement of Jesus, then Jesus would have differentiated between healings and demon exorcisms (as already in Matt. 11:5 f). To the advice of some Pharisees that he leave the realm of Herod Antipas (including Galilee), Jesus answers (Luke 13:32): "Go and tell that fox, 'Behold, I cast out demons and perform cures today and tomorrow, and the third day I finish my course.' " Jesus' activity is characterized both by demon exorcisms *and* healings. The two activities are not simply identical, as their separate mention seems to show. Accordingly, the demonological understanding of sickness would be ascribed to the demon exorcisms ("cases of possession"), while sickness as proximity to death covers the specially mentioned "healings" in Luke 13:32 and Matthew 11:5 f. The restoration of the withered or lame hand in Mark 3:1-6 would be a historical example of those "healings"; a demonological explanation of that lameness is, however, not implied in the text.

Jesus viewed only the demon exorcisms expressly as an eschatological realization of the kingdom of God (Luke 11:20). The threat of illness was overcome here on the basis of God's new, final salvation activity, and the belief in demons lost its existential power over man. However, with sickness considered more as a threatening proximity to death, such as in the case of Mark 3:1-6, the healing, and thus the struggle against sickness, appears to have been viewed from a particular perspective. In

verse 4 Jesus aims at saving the sick person and strengthening his
life. Man in this context is viewed as a creature of God. A rabbinic
principle is helpful here (Sanh. 4:5; similarly Aboth RN 31)[28]:

> For this reason Adam was created as the only one, in order to
> teach you that one (God) reckons to each person who destroys
> a soul (i.e., a human life) the same as if he had destroyed an
> entire world, and that one reckons to each person who saves a
> soul the same *as if he saved an entire world.*

Mark 3:4 also speaks about saving a "soul," or a person, and about
destroying him. The creation-theological horizon is what is
significant in the rabbinic parallels: one man is worth as much as
the entire work of creation. Are we now justified in employing
these Jewish texts, with their high evaluation of man as a creature
of God, in our interpretation of Mark 3:4? Probably yes. This
principle is characteristic for Jesus (Mark 2:27): "The Sabbath
was made for man, not man for the Sabbath." Just as God's other
creation works, the Sabbath, too, is created for man's well-being.
All of creation stands at man's service. In order to demonstrate
this to the people of his time and thus to bring the creator God's
salvation will closer to them, Jesus broke the Sabbath in a
provocative fashion when it was a matter of saving a sick person
from the realm of death (Mark 3:4). Seen against this
comprehensive background, Jesus' conviction becomes clear.
Certainly it is allowed, indeed it is commanded to save a sick
person on the Sabbath, since the Sabbath was created by God for
the sake of man. Sickness, as the threat of death, contradicts the
creator God's salvation will. In the time of the inbreaking
kingdom of God, Jesus shows by means of his healings that
sickness as a power of misfortune is conquered. The Jewish
understanding of sickness as proximity to death loses its
life-threatening nature with Jesus. On the basis of faith in the
salvation God, who, according to Jesus' conviction, is preparing
for the assumption of his final reign, he can break through the
Jewish viewpoint by showing their invalidity through his
concrete healings.

4. Sickness as the Consequence of Sin

From the Jewish tradition (cf. NT I.2) we learned that, in addition to the demonological view of sickness, one other particular conception dominated Judaism: sickness as consequential punishment for sins. The question now arises whether we can learn something about how Jesus viewed this attitude, which so burdened daily life. Judaism was in danger here of becoming decidedly cruel out of reasons of piety. The sick, suffering person was not only seriously affected by his affliction, but was also confronted with the religious condemnation experienced because of that affliction. People believed they could determine from a person's affliction that he was guilty; indeed, they believed they could even determine the kind of guilt.

We have an important statement from Jesus directing itself against the reckoning of guilt and punishment (Luke 13:1-5). To be sure, it is not here a matter of sickness as the consequence of sin, but rather of other instances of misfortune considered to be consequential punishment. Nonetheless, Jesus' position in Luke 13:1-5 permits the conclusion that he also opposed the practical consequences of that recompensatory faith in the case of sickness.

People tell Jesus about Galilean pilgrims whom Pilate had killed during sacrifice. The Galileans' fate provokes the question of whether they were particuarly sinful. Those eighteen people who died when the tower in Siloam fell were in a similar situation. Jesus answers (Luke 13:2 f): "Do you think that these Galileans were worse sinners than all the other Galileans, because they suffered thus? I tell you, No; but unless you repent you will all likewise perish."

Here, as in the following answer in Luke 13:4 f, Jesus rejects the dogma that misfortune is punishment for specific individual sins. However, he is not concerned with a theoretical dispute, but rather with the struggle against the practical consequences of this religious view. A person not affected by a particular misfortune might, in this secure conviction, consider himself not to be a sinner and thus not in need of conversion. Against that

Jesus speaks the threat: All are sinners, thus the conversion of all is necessary in view of God's impending judgment of destruction. The question concerning the guilt of those Jews who perished is settled by the reference to the catastrophe threatening the listeners. Jesus has the freedom to reject the dominant recompensatory thinking because it could lead to self-righteousness in those who were not affected by misfortune.

Did Jesus also struggle against this understanding of sickness as consequential punishment? Perhaps he did so because in its consequences the sick person's suffering was increased by adding to the physical damage, religious condemnation by the person's contemporaries. The question is difficult to answer because of the lack of reliable sources. One text might help us farther here, the healing of the man blind from birth in John 9:1 ff. Jesus rejects the question of the disciples, "Rabbi, who sinned, this man or his parents, that he was born blind?" (vv 2 and 3a), and heals the sick man (vv 6 f). This removes the oppressive problem of sin and sickness from the sick person's world. Of course, the objection against the use of this narrative is immediately raised that all the miracle stories reflect the thinking of the early Christian narrators rather than that of Jesus. Even if we can reconstruct an earlier pro-Johannine version (perhaps vv 1, 2, 3a, 6, 7), this earlier form also displays characteristics of an advanced stage in the New Testament miracle tradition, since it—as do the other healing stories in the gospel of John—gives preference to extremely difficult cases in order to let Jesus' power shine all the more brightly.

5. Historical Reminiscence Regarding Jesus' Healings in the Miracle Stories

Let us try in a preliminary fashion to inquire into other miracle stories regarding the extent to which they have preserved Jesus' understanding of sickness. We immediately come to a negative conclusion affecting all of Jesus' miracle stories. Precisely that which is characteristic of Jesus' understanding, namely the eschatologically interpreted removal of sickness as a sign of the inbreaking kingdom of God, is missing completely. As our discussion of the miracle stories will show more specifically, we find in them a tendency to strip away that which is characteristic, thus making it difficult to gain access to any relevant historical reminiscence regarding Jesus' view of sickness.

The story about the healing of Peter's mother-in-law (Mark 1:29-31) is an exception of sorts. To be sure, this narrative, too, contains schematically traditional characteristics which generally appear in miracle stories: scenic preparation (Jesus comes), healing gesture (Jesus takes the sick woman by the hand, cf. Mark 5:41; 9:27; lifts her up, cf. 2:9, 11; 3:3; 5:41; 9:27; and 10:49), confirmation of the miracle ("the fever left her") and a demonstration of the healing ("and she served them"). However, this miracle account is different from the others in that it displays details that are no longer simply topical, but that rather appear to be biographical. The story has an interest in the fact that Jesus comes into *Simon's* house and that it is *Simon's mother-in-law* who lies sick. This rather unexciting story was probably transmitted only because it dealt with Simon's mother-in-law. The biographical direction probably accounts for the fact that Jesus is not christologically profiled here (e.g., by an acclamation of the great miracle worker). This account lacks the general tendency toward a heightening in the miracle stories wich transcends the historical and factual. It might possibly contain historically reliable reminiscence rendered possible by the narrator's biographical, rather than his christological, interest.

Even though this story allows a certain access to the historical figure of Jesus, the fundamental orientation toward Simon Peter (his house, his mother-in-law) appears simultaneously to have prevented learning more about Jesus and thus about his understanding of healing. The text portrays the sickness in the briefest fashion: The woman lay sick of a fever. That fever is probably understood demonically, as suggested by the formulation alluding to demonic retreat: "And the fever left her." This is further supported by the fact that in the surrounding world, and certainly also in Judaism, a demonological understanding of fever was customary: "The increase in body temperature encouraged one in the case of a fever to trace the fever back to the effect of an extra-human force."[29] However, this view of fever in Mark 1:30 f is first of all a product of this short story's narrator and does not lead us immediately to the historical Jesus. The historical inquiry thus cannot get beyond the simple conclusion that Jesus in all probability healed a fever in Simon Peter's mother-in-law. We cannot be sure just how this healing was actually carried out, since the details in the healing portrayal correspond to the traditional schema of such healings and thus do not allow any conclusion concerning Jesus' particular therapy. Any conjectures concerning the nature of the fever remain pure speculation. This holds true for a diagnosis of malaria resulting from the damp climate on the Sea of Galilee, as well as for the conjecture of delirious conditions of hysteria which temporarily affect the sick person and make a sudden healing possible.

In addition to Mark 1:29-31, the story about blind Bartimaeus can claim a certain historical foundation (Mark 10:46-52). Again, certain biographically singular details support this: The spatially bound nature of the story (Jericho) and the name of the person healed (Bartimaeus). However, the narrative's historical resources are already at an end with the factual healing of a blind person. We cannot tell from the story what kind of eye illness was involved, and just as little can we conclude anything concerning Jesus' interpretation of this illness.

In view of all these observations we can conclude the following: "It is beyond question that Jesus was active in exorcism; we simply do not have any authentic individual account of this activity. It is equally certain that Jesus healed sick people, but we only know about a few individual cases (the healing of fever, of blindness, of a lame hand, for example) which can be historically secured. Beyond this we are not even in a position as regards these cases to diagnose the presupposed illness medically and to describe more precisely Jesus'—certainly charismatic and not medical—practice of healing."[30] To this evaluation we can only add the observation that Jesus' own view of healing has been preserved only in transmitted statements (particularly Luke 11:20 and Mark 3:4). The miracle stories no longer allow us to learn just how his eschatological conviction led to the overcoming of the misfortune sickness entailed.

III. Frequent Sickness in the New Testament Miracle Stories

The character of individual sickness can, in the New Testament, only be described on the basis of the thorough portrayals in the miracle stories, though here, too, the modern reader encounters tight limitations. These stories deal with sicknesses only to the extent that they thus create a background and prerequisite for the great healing act of the various miracle workers (usually Jesus). They are thus not interested in sickness as such. Information about the sicknesses is accordingly sparse. Furthermore, we encounter these largely in a mythological language not allowing an exact diagnosis in the modern sense.

1. Possession

When we speak here about possession, we are referring to manifestations of sickness that were perceived as being particularly agonizing and whose healing the sick person or the people around him longed for. This does not include cases of being filled with God, religiously productive conditions that were virtually sought after. Pythia thus felt possessed by the god Apollo and was able to give oracles. In another way, charismatic figures in Israel experienced how the spirit of Yahweh came over them and enabled them to perform special acts before the people (e.g., Judges 3:10; 1 Sam. 11:6).

During the time of early Christianity, Palestine was overrun with an enormous tide of possession phenomena. The large number of reports in the gospels are already testimony to this. The sick person, as well as the people around him, viewed this suffering as the terrible surrender to a demon who resided in the sick person and totally dominated him. The person lost his own subjectivity and became void of will, an object of the "unclean spirit." The gospel accounts, as well as heathen descriptions, agree that whenever the sick person speaks or performs violent acts, it is not he who does this, but rather the demon dwelling within him.

There have been attempts to explain the high frequency of possession cases during precisely that period. Palestine had for a long time undergone foreign political domination and thus, social and cultural oppression. Foreign political domination was, for Jewish understanding, *eo ipso* associated with the concept of the reign of foreign gods or demons. In the case of an appropriate disposition in man, the external experience of powerlessness encountered in the face of this double oppression could be transferred to the interior. The "demonic curse," which was finally experienced as forced physical kind of social-psychological interpretation of possession by comparing Palestinian conditions with those in other cultures: "From the shamanism of Siberian tribes we know that, in a milieu of strong inter-ethnic pressure, manifestations of possession by spirits play a particularly important role. 'Oppression' by a foreign, dominating people can appear enciphered as 'possession' by a foreign (of foreign origin) spirit. Something similar also holds true for the situation of Judaism during the time of Jesus. It had been preceded by centuries of foreign domination and oppression. The Maccabean revolt against Hellenistic inundation was only a few generations old, and Roman domination was even younger. That kind of thing has a demonizing effect. . . ."[31]

Fear of demons and with it the fear of demonic infection by possessed people was great at that time. It was heightened particularly because of the lack of sequestered institutions; manifestations of possession occurred openly in public. Thus Mark 1:23 ff also describes how a sick person begins convulsing in the middle of the synagogue (v 26). The church father Hieronymous tells us in A.D. 401 about a pilgrimage to Palestine made by a certain Paula in A.D. 385 (Epistle 108). She saw how in Samaria the deranged were concentrated in public near the saintly graves of the prophets Elisha, Obadiah, and John the Baptist:

> She (Paula) trembled there in the face of many astonishing experiences. She saw namely how demons bellowed under all sorts of torments and how men howled before the graves of the saints like wolves, how they barked like dogs, snorted like lions, hissed like snakes, bellowed like steers, and how others hurled their heads around and touched the ground backwards with their crown.

In this portrayal we already encounter the decisive characteristic marking these manifestations of possession. The sick people no longer had control of themselves, but were rather subjected—according to the understanding of the time—to demons.

a) The suppression of one's own subjectivity finds expression in ancient reports particularly in the fact that the sick person is no longer speaking, but rather the demon dwelling within him:

> And the sick person no longer has his own voice, but rather speaks heavily and hollow, like the man; he looks more with strange eyes than with his own. (Philostratus, *Life of Apollonius* III, 38)

> . . . the sick person himself is silent, but the demon answers in Greek or in a foreign language.   (Lucian, *Friend of Lies*, 16)

We encounter this same characteristic in the exorcisms in Mark 1:21-28 and 5:1-20. In Mark 1:21-28 a man with an "unclean spirit" meets the miracle worker, Jesus. The "unclean spirit" senses Jesus' presence and begins the battle with an outcry (24): "What have you to do with *us*, Jesus of Nazareth? Have you come to destroy *us*?" It is noticeable that the demon, and not really the sick person himself, cries out. He uses the mouth of the sick person, who is only a tool without a will. This is shown by the plural "us," which indicates that several demons are the actual subject in the sick person. We find the plural in the defense formulation: "What have you to do with us?" as well as in the following statement which recognizes Jesus as the destroyer of the demon world.

Mark 5:1-20 portrays something much the same as the

previous text. After the characterization of the sickness as madness (vv 3b-4) with a strong tendency toward self-destruction (v 5), that typical characteristic of possession finds expression again: the loss of one's own personal center to the demonic power. This power, and not the sick person himself, cries out to ward off the miracle worker (v 7). It again becomes clear that several demons are dwelling within the sick person, since to the question "What is your name?" the adversary answers: "My name is Legion; for we are many" (v 9). Accordingly, it becomes clear in the following verses 10-13 that it is an entire army of demons.

b) The possessed person no longer controls his own actions; the demonic power does: "It is not you who are doing this wickedness, but rather the demon who controls you without your knowing" (Philostratus, *Life of Apollonius* IV 20). Not only does the spirit suppress the sick person's own possibility of decision, he even attempts to destroy it: "But he threatens with unhanging and splitting, and with the killing of my son" (*Life of Apollonius* III 38). This destructive effectiveness of the demon to whom the sick person is given over, finds terrifying expression particularly in Mark 9:14-29. The sick person is a mere object of the demon's destructive fury (vv 18, 20, 22). The father reports the following about the previous course of his son's illness:

> And wherever it seizes him, it dashes him down; and he foams and grinds his teeth and becomes rigid. (v 18) And it has often cast him into the fire and into the water, to destroy him. (v 22)

Among the New Testament reports, Mark 5:1-20 and 9:14-29 also offer symptoms of more individual illnesses in addition to the typical characteristics of possession we have pointed out up till now, thus enabling us to differentiate between the various reports. The astonishing state of affairs is that the prerequisites for a diagnosis in the modern sense appear just in these cases of possession. This is striking since these possibilities are generally sparse within the New Testament sickness stories; the popular narrative employs the ancient world's mythological way of viewing things. Here, however, the presentation appears to be based to a large extent on actual observation and allows us to outline a diagnosis of the illness, although the narrative to a large degree employs the demonological categories of current descriptions of illness.

The story in Mark 5:1 ff describes a serious case of madness in verses 3-4. Although they try to bind the demoniac with fetters and chains and thus subdue him, it does not work because he breaks everything apart. Verse 5 adds (cf. already v 3*a*) that he lives among the tombs and on the mountains, is always crying out and bruising himself with stones. This tendency toward self-punishment points to a strong self-destructive urge.

The entire portrayal corresponds to the experiences they had with possessed people at that time. We accordingly read in the Palestinian Talmud[32]: "The characteristics of a madman: whenever someone runs out at night, whenever he sleeps overnight among graves, and whenever he destroys what one gives him." These individual characteristics, which to a large extent agree with the description in Mark 5, are already typical within certain parameters. The Gerasene demoniac thus does not just represent an individual case, but rather also reflects the usual image of particular cases of possession in Palestine at that time. Nonetheless, an acute psychotic condition can be recognized here in outline with the main symptoms of delirium, destructive fury, and the inclination toward self-destruction.

If we look at Mark 9:14-29 more closely, we discover a different image of sickness than in Mark 1:21-28 and Mark 5:1-20. We notice first that the suppression of human subjectivity is not viewed the same way here as in the previous cases. There it was emphasized that the "unclean spirit" was speaking from within the person (cf. the plural, which indicates several spirits, Mark 1:24 and 5:9, 10, 12); here this characteristic is missing entirely. The following observations are significant. The sick person is helplessly given over to the "spirit's" arbitrary will, and is coerced into destructive reactions. To be sure, this feature is generally quite typical for cases of possession. However, the portrayal in Mark 9:14 ff displays some peculiar elements.

The affliction appears only to occur at intervals. The spirit "seizes" the boy (v 18). "And when the spirit saw him [Jesus], immediately it convulsed the boy, and he fell on the ground and rolled about, foaming at the mouth" (v 20). Then Jesus poses the following question as if raising an anamnesis: "How long has he had this?" (v 21). The father's answer then reveals that since childhood the sick boy has often been thrown into fire or water and thus had his life endangered (v 22). In contrast to the Gerasene in Mark 5:1 ff, the sick boy apparently lives with his father; his affliction does not dominate him so constantly that he must live secluded like the Gerasene: "*Night and day* among the tombs and on the mountains . . ." (Mark 5:5). The Gerasene's delirium is not just seen in individual attacks, but rather in the constant, lasting inclination toward madness, in the face of which they were not able to bind and thus subdue him (5:3*b*-4). The pecularities in the description of the illness in 9:14 ff, which agree with contemporary observations today, allow us to conclude the presence of epileptic attacks. The spirit "seizes" the boy, "dashes" him down, the sick boy "foams at the mouth," "grinds his teeth," and "becomes rigid." Or we read: the spirit "convulses him terribly," or he lies "like a corpse." The final statement refers to the deep unconsciousness typical of epileptic attacks.

In the portrayal in 9:14 ff we notice that there is emphasis on the "dumb spirit" the sick boy has (9:17), indeed there is even talk of the "dumb and deaf spirit" which has to be exorcized (9:25). This characterization of the "spirit" fits the rest of the story only with some qualification. It is indeed characterisic of epileptic attacks that the sick person cannot speak or be spoken to, but these manifestations only accompany the attack, and are not such dominant symptoms that they occur outside the attack. When, however, the spirit dominating the sick boy is characterized as "dumb and deaf" (9:17, 25), this is not only referring to an additional condition of the demon which corresponds to a secondary manifestation of the illness, but rather to its primary characteristic; it points to an ongoing condition of sickness consisting in deafness and speechlessness. This differentiated state of affairs leads to the conclusion that, in Mark 9:14 ff, two quite different images of sickness are interwoven: deafness and speechlessness, and epilepsy.[33] This thesis finds support in the literary or historical-critical problems of the entire narrative. Not only do two images of sickness appear to be mixed here, but the other problem is that various levels can be differentiated that suggest that the story has a growth history. The characterization of the spirit as "dumb and deaf" can be attributed to the evangelist's redactional additions; in contrast to Jesus' healing activity (Mark 7:37)—"He has done all things well; he even makes the deaf hear and the dumb speak"—he formulates a negative characterization of the "spirit."

The other two Gospel writers who retold Mark 9:14-29 possibly consciously noticed the incongruence of the description of the illness. In any case, there is no mention of a "dumb and deaf spirit" in Matthew 17:14-20 or Luke 9:37-43. The two Gospel writers only took up those features that point to epilepsy, and in Matthew, this has been carried through with great consistency. He describes the sick boy as "epileptic" (as a lunatic, from lunar, moon; 17:15). This is explained by the ancient view that the occurrence of epileptic attacks is dependent upon the phases of the moon. Thus we read for example in Lucian (*The Friend of Lies*) about a Syrian from Palestine who heals possessed people by exorcism: "He takes up those who are given to the moon, who roll their eyes and foam at the mouth, so that they stand up, and he releases them healthy."

A brief overview of Greek views is necessary in order to fit the early Christian evaluation of epilepsy into its contemporary environment.[34] Popular understanding called epilepsy the "holy sickness" (first documented in Heraclitus and Herodotus). The sick were not supposed to appear as saints or prophets, but rather as marked in some special way by the gods. The sickness was imposed, for example, as punishment for past sins. The author of the writing "On the Holy Sickness," contained in the Hippocratic collection, rejects this diagnosis from an enlightened perspective and orders epilepsy among all the other sicknesses, which he attempts to explain empirically-scientifically. He emphasizes, as regards epilepsy (chapter 1): "It appears to me no more divine or holy than the other sicknesses, but rather has the same source as the others."

In spite of rational diagnoses and therapy in Greek medicine, the supernatural interpretation in the demonological

sense remained the dominant Hellenistic view, and this had
catastrophic consequences for the social position of the epileptic.
Because epileptics were believed to be possessed by demons,
people were afraid of them, be it that an attack was considered to
be a bad omen, be it that one was afraid of becoming tainted or
even that the demon might gain power over one. People tried to
ward off the demon by means of spitting as a figurative gesture
(cf. Gal. 4:13 f). The result was that an epileptic fled to a secluded
place when an attack was imminent. If no cure was found, his life
was filled with shame, insults, and torment.[35]

The early Christian view is shaped by the fact that Christ
came to liberate the possessed from the demons controlling
them. Exorcism "in the name of Jesus" was considered the only
possible cure (Mark 16:17). Otherwise a two-fold distinction can
be made concerning the heathen view. In the first place, the
Christians never adopted the view of epilesy as a "holy sickness,"
but rather ordered it among the other manifestations of
possession. In the second place, in the fathers of the ancient
church we find a conscious rejection of the empirical interpretation of epilepsy in the sense of its interpretation by Greek
medicine. The attempt at an empirical-rational manner of
observation is unmistakable there, even if it was not completely
scientific in the modern sense; for example, when the origin of
epilepsy was thought to be a variation of the brain's consistency
because of the influence of cold, sun, and wind, which then led to
a clogging of the brain's receptacles. This path was cut off from
the ancient church for a long time. Origen's position here had a
lasting effect (*Commentary to Matthew* 13:8):

> Physicians may nonetheless attempt a natural explanation (of
> the illness), since in their opinion there is no unclean spirit at
> work here, but rather a manifestation of sickness of the body.
> In their natural explanation they may assert that the moisture
> moves about in the head according to a certain sympathy with
> the light of the moon, which itself is of a moist nature. We,
> however, also believe according to the gospel that this illness
> in those affected is caused, as is well known, by an unclean
> dumb and deaf spirit.

The biblical text Mark 9:14-29, with its characterization of the "spirit," had a special after-effect here.

2. So-called Leprosy

Skin diseases carrying the name "leprosy" were frequent in Palestine in New Testament times. Accordingly, they are exhaustively treated in the rabbinic tradition. To be sure, it is difficult to determine just which diseases are really meant by the Greek word *lepra* (Hebrew *ṣara ' at*). Regarding historical orientation, the following holds true. The legal determinations (particularly Lev. 13 f), as well as the other accounts of "leprosy" in the Old Testament, hardly refer to leprosy in the modern sense, i.e., to the infectious disease whose bacteria was discovered (1868) and described (1872) by the Norwegian physician Hansen (cf. OT III.1). As a matter of fact, ancient reports appear to indicate that the armies of Alexander the Great were the first to bring this disease into the Mediterranean area from India.[36] Thus Pliny the Elder reports to us (*History of Nature* 267) that leprosy in Italy was only first spread by the legions of Pompey.

As a Greek word for actual leprosy we find *elephantiasis* (in Celsus 25 B.C.-A.D. 37, in Pliny the Elder and Galen, born A.D. 128/129), while the word *lepra* in the Hippocratic writings, as well as later, would sooner correspond to modern-day psoriasis.[37] When the Greek translation of the Old Testament, the Septuagint, uses the word *lepra* as a rendering for the Hebrew term *ṣara ' at*, it therefore does not appear to mean leprosy in the modern sense in the skin diseases described in the Old Testament. This conclusion does have significance for the New Testament understanding. If the word *lepra* in general Greek usage—which also influenced the Greek rendering of the Old Testament—does not mean leprosy in the modern sense, then it is extremely difficult to consider actual leprosy to be the disease meant in the New Testament accounts of "leprosy." It is certainly possible that cases of actual leprosy, in certain stages similar to the Greek *lepra* (psoriasis or other skin diseases), were designated with this term. Thus we cannot exclude the possibility that the New Testament designation *lepra* did refer to actual leprosy. Nonetheless, language usage sooner suggests other skin diseases.

If one looks at the Jewish statements concerning ṣara ' at or *lepra*, we find the real suffering in the fact that it made one cultically impure. The exclusion of the "leper" from the community did not result from hygienic considerations involving the danger of infection, but rather came about because the "leprosy" endangered the theocratic holiness of the whole people. "For a leper, according to rabbinic views, did not just contaminate (ritually) whatever he touched, but rather his mere entrance into a house contaminated everything in it, indeed one could under certain conditions become contaminated through a chance encounter with him, for example, under a tree."[38] This view isolated the sick person from human company. Josephus reports accordingly that "lepers" had to go about alone and with torn clothing out of doors (*Contra Apion* K 31). Even if his assertion that they had to avoid not only the city of Jerusalem, but all villages as well, does not quite correspond to actual circumstances, the rigor of such separation is terrible enough. It is thus quite comprehensible that, according to opinion at that time, the existence of "lepers" was in no respect different from that of dead people (Josephus, *Jewish Antiquities* III 11,3). We then read:[39] "Four are considered the equal of a dead person: the poor, the leprous, the blind, and the childless." The quality of life of "lepers" was socially and religiously diminished in such a way that they belonged more to the domain of death than to life. Accordingly, the healing of a leper was considered equal with the raising of the dead, and according to rabbinic understanding, it is as difficult as the raising of the dead.[40] It is only possible as a healing by God. Should a sick person be healed, the priest must expressly declare the healed person pure. Only then is he permitted to resume his normal position in human company.

Let us now look at the New Testament accounts of leprosy healing. Of the transmitted passages (Matt. 11:5 par. Luke 7:22; Matt. 10:8; Luke 4:27; cf. 14:3) only the first has particular significance. In it we find leprosy healings as signs of the inbreaking time of salvation, which is depicted with ready, traditional images without appearing to trace back the leprosy healings to the contents of transmitted prophesies of the salvation period (cf. NT II.3). They could thus be a reflection of the reality of the historical Jesus. In Matthew 10:8 we have the instruction to the disciples to perform miracles. However, as regards the mention of leprosy healings, the passage is not an independent transmission; this information appears to have been added by the evangelist from Matthew 11:5 to an extant shorter instruction passage (cf. the pars. Luke 9:2). In Luke 4:27 there is only indirect mention of possible miracles Jesus performed on lepers. More descriptions, which are the only ones we will look at more closely, are found in the stories in Mark 1:40-45 and Luke 17:11-19.

The pre-Markan version of the present story in Mark 1:40-45 which the evangelist found before him, encompasses approximately verses 40-44, while at very least verse 45 comes from the pen of the evangelist who emphasizes the revelation of Jesus' deed. What view of sickness does this pre-Markan text already have? We notice first that the person seeking healing *approaches* Jesus and expresses his request for healing while on his knees (v 40). According to the postscript of the law (Lev. 13:45 f), the "leper" has to cry out from a distance "unclean, unclean" in order to avoid the danger of contaminating others in an encounter. The text, however, does not concern itself with that. There is apparently supposed to be a direct meeting with the miracle worker Jesus. The wording of the request is important: "If you will, you can make me clean." Jesus' command corresponds to it and, with the power-transmitting touch of the hand, effects the healing (v 41): "I will; be clean." With his trusting request "if you will" the "leper" confesses Jesus' divine power, and Jesus confirms this with the formulation of the command. Otherwise one can only say of God that he can do whatever he wills. God created everything according to his will (Ps. 115:3; 135:6); he does everything he wants (Eccles. 8:3); he can carry through whenever he wills (Wis. 12:18). In Mark 1:40 this divine power is transferred to Jesus, and this is what is really of interest in this story. It is christologically directed. It attributes to Jesus a deed that is otherwise reserved for God, in order to emphasize his character as a divine power: "The narrator no doubt means incurable leprosy which can only be cured by God. However, with this 'opinion' he is not offering a medical diagnosis, but posits rather a kerygmatic point of departure which cannot be secured as a historical fact. The leper is one of those 'dead people' who will experience salvation in the end time."[41] The incurable nature of the disease is here a theological interpretive category with which the greatness of Jesus' miracle is described.

Another feature of the healing story goes in this direction. It is apparent that the word "cleanse" here encompasses the meaning "to heal." This implies two things. First, it shows that it is precisely that contaminating effect of "leprosy" from which the sick person is to be cleansed, i.e., healed. Second, we can see that Jesus does not just act in the sense of declaring the person pure, as the priest according to Leviticus 13 f is to do (cf. Mark 1:44). He effects the healing itself, as the confirmation of the success of the healing shows (v 42); "And immediately the leprosy left him, and he was made clean."

The usage of the term "to cleanse" is probably based here on the model of the Old Testament text 2 Kings 5, where the Syrian, Naaman, is made clean, i.e., healed by the prophet Elisha (5:10, 12, 13, 14; cf. OT II. 4; III.1). Jesus thus appears as a prophet, probably as a prophet of the eschaton who is greater than Elisha, since one can confess of him, as of God: "If you will, you can make me clean."

In the confirmation of the successful healing (v 42) we see suggested that the "leprosy," like the fever in Mark 1:31, is thought to be caused by a demon; or only fever and leprosy appear in the New Testament as diseases which befall man like a demon and then leave him again. Nonetheless, the narrative does not have the character of an exorcism story, since the healing is performed by means of power transferral and command, and not by the express exorcism of a demon.

All these individual features show clearly that the narrator discusses this disease in terms of religious categories of understanding. He offers no protocol of a leprosy healing, but rather proclaims Jesus as the powerful Lord who remains victorious also over "leprosy." He employs in the background a view of this disease according to which it is demonically caused. But we learn nothing about the empirical condition of the intended disease, nothing about the precise nature of the physical damage associated with it. Defining the designated skin disease as "leprosy" would be ignoring the text.

The story about the healing of the ten lepers in Luke 17:11-19 is even more reserved concerning the nature of the disease. Actually, only the first part of the narrative, verses 11-14, comes into question, and in them we find an extremely brief healing story. The second part no longer deals with sickness and healing, but rather with the contrast between the gratefulness of the one Samaritan and ingratitude of the nine Jews. In the healing narrative in verses 11-14 there are ten "lepers." When they encounter Jesus, they remain—as is in accord with Jewish law (Lev. 13:45 f)—at a distance and call out to Jesus (vv 12 f). The disease is thus presupposed, quite traditionally, to have a contaminating nature. Jesus reacts to their pleas. To be sure, he does not speak a command that brings about healing, and does not touch the sick men either, in order to give them the power of health as is portrayed in Mark 1:41. He only instructs them to show themselves to the priests for the purpose of ascertaining purity (v 14). This challenge is probably thought of as a test of faith. Because they leave immediately after his words, trusting him, they become clean on the way to the priests (v 14b). Just as in Mark 1:40 ff, cleansing here means being healed from the disease. This addresses the decisive aspect of the disease, the contaminating nature of "leprosy." Then, according to the prescripts of the law, the determination of purity by the priest must follow the healing; only this allows the healed person to return to normal society. It is clear that in this story in Luke 17:11-19 the view of "leprosy" stays completely within the framework of Jewish understanding. We do not learn anything further about the nature of this disease beyond the mention of its contaminating effect. A medical diagnosis cannot be attempted.

3. Blindness

Blindness was a widespread phenomenon in antiquity in the southern Mediterranean countries.[42] Inheritance was thought to be the cause of blindness, both for those blind from birth, as well as for those in whom it appeared during the course of life. Blindness was traced back to poisoning, to injuries in accidents, or to the consequences of diseases such an eye inflammation. In addition, psychological causes such as grief and tears are mentioned.

Particularly noticeable in blind people was their unsteady walk. The blind person stretched out his hands to find support, and used a staff to guide his feet. Their social situation was normally a terrible one. Even if there were rich blind people, most lived in great poverty because most professions were closed to them. A typical image was thus the blind beggar.

In general, blindness was considered one of the most serious fates, since the Greeks thought the eye to be the main organ, whose loss meant great suffering. In spite of the occasional opinion that blindness sharpened one's spiritual vision, and that only the blind could be poets, it remained a hard fate.

Blindness was considered virtually incurable. People were generally convinced that, not medical arts, but only the power of a divinely favored miracle worker or a god could bring about healing. Even the healing of Vespasian's blindness appears to be a miracle pointing to the "favor of heaven" and a "certain inclination of the gods toward Vespasian" (Tacitus, *Histories* IV 81). The description of the specific conditions surrounding this healing is illuminating. Vespasian is at first reluctant to go through with the healing he requested. He demands "a physician's confirmation" that such blindness "can be healed by human help." The physicians answer elusively. Their opinion is then: "Perhaps the gods are concerned, and perhaps he, the prince, is elected to be a tool of the deity" (Tacitus, ibid.). The difficulty of healing blindness also becomes clear in the fact that no such healings are reported of the great miracle worker, Apollonius of Tyana. However, what presents difficulties even for a miracle worker, succeeds with the gods. Such miracles are reported particularly in the case of Aesculapius (e.g., Miracles Nr. 4, 18, 65). We read the following about a blind person who undergoes temple sleep (Miracle 18): "This one was blind and saw a dream; he dreamed that the god came to him and opened his eyes with his fingers, and then he saw the trees in the sanctuary for the first time. When day came, he came out healthy."

The Jews also considered blindness to be a great suffering. People were convinced "there was no greater grief and no greater or more serious suffering" than blind eyes (Midrash Ps. 146:8). The hard fate of the blind becomes clear in the comparison of his condition with that of a dead person.[43] On the basis of the sin-punishment association, blindness appears as God's punishment for past misdeeds. Man is punished in the organ with which he has sinned; thus blindness occurs as the result of lasciviousness of the eyes. The situation of the blind beggar was also typical for Judaism. Whoever cries out "Give to the blind" as a blind person, i.e., whoever imitates a blind person, will finally become blind himself.[44]

In general, Judaism did not expect any healing. One figured on it only in extraordinary cases. Thus the angel Raphael ordered therapy for the blind Tobit which led to healing by means of the use of fish gall (Tob. 11:7 ff). It is said of the Amorites, who to a large extent were considered magicians, that a particular glowing stone would heal one if one's eyes were placed on it (Ps.-Philo., *Biblical Antiquities* 25,12). The healing missed in the present was hoped for in the eschatological future[45]: "Everything God has struck in this world he will one day heal again. Thus the blind will be healed." "When he comes to heal the world, he will first heal the blind."

The New Testament took the distressing fate of the blind seriously and did not just envision a future solution to their problem. Commensurate with experiential reality of the period, we encounter the blind person as a beggar (Mark 10:46; John 9:8). Begging was the only possibility of getting through life. Commensurate with the common situation of distress, the blind were mentioned together with the deaf and lame (Matt. 11:5; 15:30; 21:24; Luke 14:21). There is hardly any reflection at all about the origin of blindness and thus about possible causes of blindness. Because of the lack of exegetical supports, any diagnosis such as nervous or functional disturbances in the eyes is superfluous.[46] The suddenness of the healing, for example, in Mark 10:52, is a typical feature of Hellenistic miracle narratives and does not yet permit the conclusion that we are dealing with nonorganic eyes injuries. The texts do not explain blindness in an empirical-rational fashion, but rather ask, if at all, about its religious etiology. In John 9:1 we learn that the blind person has been suffering "since birth." The disciples try to find out whether he or his parents sinned and caused the blindness (John 9:2). Behind this lies the Jewish view that the parents' guilt is avenged on the children. It does not, however, become clear to what extent the person born blind himself could have sinned, whether as a child in the womb (according to various rabbinic statements) or whether God's foresight made him be born blind (because of a knowledge of future sins). In any case, behind the disciples' question in John 9:2 stands a manner of thinking coming from the context of "sin, and sickness as a consequent punishment." The cause of blindness is seen differently in what follows. The blind person in Matthew 12:22, who is also deaf, experienced this fate because of demonic injury. In Acts 13:11 the magician Bar Jesus is blinded as punishment. It is caused by a curse and occurs immediately after the curse is spoken.

In Matthew 11:5 and Luke 7:22 the healings of blindness are considered with other miracles as signs of the salvation period commencing with Jesus' proclamation of the kingdom of God (cf. also Luke 4:18). Blindness healings are described more thoroughly in the miracle stories in Mark 8:22-26 and John 9:1 ff. The accounts, in large measure, follow the model of the Hellenistic miracle narrative in which the healing transfer of power occurs through touch (Mark 8:23, 25) and healing substances (spittle: Mark 8:23; John 9:6). This also indicates that blindness is understood as a condition of bodily weakness or as lack of vital power which can only be alleviated by a supernatural tranfer of power (cf. NT IV.2). In Mark 10:46-52, these means of therapy are missing, since the story concentrates on the blind person's believing trust in Jesus, which effects the healing (10:52).

4. Paralysis

For this subtitle we have chosen as general a designation as possible that can encompass the phenomena in question; so-called lameness and other impairments of movement. Since a medical diagnosis seems impossible in most cases, this procedure is necessary to avoid being under an illusion about the determination of the various afflictions because of a one-sided use of the terms "lameness" or "paralysis." Forms of movement incapacity can be found quite frequently in the New Testament. This also holds true in the Greek realm as the miracle healings in Epidaurus testify. Similar to the appearance of the person seeking help in Mark 2:3, we read there: "N. N. of Epidaurus, lame. He came into the sanctuary as a supplicant on a litter" (Miracle 35); or "Demosthenes from X, with lame legs. He came into the sanctuary on a litter and went about supported on crutches" (Miracle 64).

Several cases of lameness treated in Epidaurus appear to be based on "neurogenic functional disturbances" that are "easily accessible to emotional healing."[47] Thus several of the sick are healed by a strengthening of the will effected by the god Aesculapius. In Miracle 35, the lame person dreams during a temple sleep that he is to climb on top of the temple by means of a ladder. He tries it, loses courage in the dream—which is a nightmare—and gives up. The god laughs at him because of his cowardice. After waking in the morning, he tries to complete the task and is suddenly healed. Miracle 37 is similar. In a dream the god orders a lame person to climb into a pond with ice-cold water. He cannot bring himself to do it, and the god chides him because of his weak trust. After waking up, however, he dares to bathe and becomes healthy.

While one can presume psychogenic afflictions in some of the cases known from Epidaurus, since the healing apparently occurred because of psychic changes, the textual prerequisites necessary for such an interpretation are missing entirely from the miracle stories in the New Testament that are concerned with the healing of the lame. The infirmity itself is only described in extremely brief terms. The description of the healing contains no features that suggest an extended procedure of strengthening the will of the sick person. This kind of interpretation is virtually excluded in Matthew 8:5 ff, where there occurs a healing, from a distance, of the lame son of the heathen centurion. A suggestive influence from Jesus to the boy is impossible here.

In characterizing the sick person's distress, which is a typical motif in the miracle stories, the various narrators emphasize how long the affliction lasts. Luke 13:10 ff deals with a woman who had had "a spirit of infirmity for eighteen years," and was so "bent over" that she could not fully straighten herself (v 11). The "paralyzed" Aeneas had been bedridden for eight years (Acts 9:33 f). The sick man at the Bethzatha pool had been ill for thirty-eight years (John 5:1 ff); and as verses 8 f suggest (cf. Mark 2:11), he is pictured as being severely impaired or lame. There are also cases of people born lame. The person lame from birth in Acts 3 always had to be carried to his begging place (v 2). As the result of the healing show, his illness consists in a "weakness" of limbs which led to the inability to walk: "And immediately his feet and ankles were made strong. And leaping up he stood and walked" (v 7). Any further diagnosis would put excessive demands on the text. It is particularly misleading to take the remark "lame from birth" (3:2) as an indication of an "endogenous condition" "as occurs in hysteria."[48] Here, as in Acts 14:8 ff, the remark concerning the duration of the suffering only expresses the seriousness of the illness. The apostle's miraculous power, which is able to perform such astonishing deeds, shines all the more brightly. The same narrative technique is at work here as in Jesus' miraculous healings. The fact that a person was born lame is only the final heightening of the other information concerning the duration of the suffering. They serve to demonstrate the power and thus the fame of the miracle worker. They are not, however, suitable for offering medical details.

Compared to the previously mentioned "lame healings," Mark 2:1 ff and 3:1 ff are relatively reserved in the description of the seriousness of the suffering. There is no mention of the duration of the illness. Nonetheless, the description of the "lame person" who must be carried to Jesus on a litter by four men, serves to emphasize the distressful situation, just as does the mention of the duration of the suffering in the other stories. It is the prerequisite for the praise of God who lets such miracles happen (Mark 2:12). Nothing can be learned about the nature of the paralysis from this, nor from the statement of forgiveness of sins by Jesus (v 5) which precedes the healing (v 11). The forgiveness of sins is not intended as a kind of "psychotherapeutic" treatment (a liberation of the sick person from an alleged feeling of guilt, which in some sense is connected with the paralysis), so that the paralysis would by inference have a psychogenic cause. The story is concerned rather with emphasizing—in the forgiveness of sins and physical healing— the full reintegration of the person into beneficial community with God.

The suffering of the man mentioned in Mark 3:1 ff is described in popular parlance. He has a "withered" hand that is probably stiff and cannot move. The basic idea here is that, just as plants die because of dryness, so also can the human body become "withered" or "consumed" by injurious causes. Accordingly, we read in Epidaurus Miracle 60 concerning a healing: "The withered (leg) became alive again." Mark 3:1 ff describes a healing of a right hand, as parallels suggest that mention the same infirmity (1 Kings 13:4; Test. Sim. 2:12). Although the story does not go into it, the social consequences of such a paralysis in the world at that time should be considered. On the basis of a continuation of the narrative in the so-called Nazarene Gospel, it becomes clear in what kind of situation the lame person found himself. The narrator imagines that the man with the "withered" hand was a mason by profession. He accordingly has him say to Jesus: "I was a mason and earned (my) keep with (my) hands; I plead to you, Jesus, to return my health to me so that I must not disgracefully beg for food." As we have already seen in the case of blindness, physical incapacity often necessitated begging (thus also in Acts 3:2).

IV. The Understanding of Sickness and Healing in the New Testament Miracle Stories

The miracle stories dealing with Jesus' exorcisms and healings received their form from early Christian narrators. These narrators molded the stories from the perspective of their own understanding of sickness, and are thus articulating their own problems here and offering solutions determined by their own faith. The motifs in the stories reveal narrative schemata that had not only formally influenced these stories in an external fashion, but also determined the content. The post-Easter community is speaking here, so that the miracle stories are documents of *their* faith, and do not represent the views of the historical Jesus.

It seems in order to divide the miracle stories in question into two main groups; those dealing with *exorcisms* and those concerned with *therapy*.[49] The collective listings of Jesus' miracles (the so-called summaries) mention exorcisms and therapy separately (Mark 1:32 f; 3:10 f; 6:13; Luke 6:18 f; 7:21; 13:32). The disciples are told to drive out demons in the name of Jesus (Mark 16:17) and to heal the sick (Mark 16:18). The demonological motifs are particularly different in the two narrative forms. In the exorcisms, the demon dwells in the sick person, and the exorcist must accordingly drive him out so that he leaves. In the therapies, the demon has only externally caused the illness. It therefore does not need to be driven out; the healing of the illness comes about by means of a transferral of power which lifts the condition of "weakness" caused by the demon. For the rest, the demonological motifs are not at all contitutive for the therapies. A demonological understanding of the sickness is often missing, while the idea of a demon dwelling within the sick person is a fundamental part of exorcisms.

This initial distinction between the two miracle types already suggests its relevance for the various views of sickness. The cause and peculiarity of the sickness is explained differently, even when demonological ideas also play a role in the therapy.

These miracle stories—exorcisms as well as therapies—follow a particular narrative schema with a relatively rigid framework of motifs that can, however, be varied in individual cases.

a) An introduction speaks about the coming of the miracle worker, the throng of spectators, and about the appearance of the person in need.

b) The exposition then directly prepares for the miracle. The characterization of the distress situation is particularly important here. Thus the duration of the illness is mentioned, its terrible or dangerous nature, and the previous futile attempts by physicians to heal it. This exposition also includes the portrayal of how those seeking help approach the miracle workers, as well as their pleas, cries for help, and expressions of trust.

c) The middle of the narrative contains the actual miracle event. The healing is effected by means of touching with the hand and healing substances (therapy) or by means of a miraculous order and threat (particularly in exorcisms). Then the success of the miracle is confirmed, particularly its abruptness.

d) The conclusion offers a demonstration that is to persuade the reader of the reality of the healing. The healed person shows his new-found vital power (therapy), the demon demonstrates his own exorcism by wreaking havoc outside the possessed person (exorcisms). The stylistically customary conclusion also includes the reaction of the public, perhaps an acclamation of the miracle worker.

If we look at the field of narrative motifs, it becomes clear at first glance that the middle part of the stories, with its portrayal of the healing, leads us to expect particular information concerning the understanding of the healing influencing the stories. Accordingly, it will be possible to draw conclusions there concerning the fundamental view of sickness influencing the healing methods (important for the therapies).

1. The Understanding of Healing in the Exorcisms

In the exorcisms we are dealing with activities in which the demon controlling the sick person is driven out in an actual struggle between the demon and the miracle workers. In the descriptions of manifestations of possession, we already saw that this illness is characterized by the suppression of the sick person's subjectivity by the demon dwelling within him. The healing can thus only be done by driving out the demon. This is the prerequisite for the restoration of the previously sick person's self-determination; he gains his ego anew.

a) In the encounter between the miracle worker and the possessed, the demon immediately senses the presence of the miracle worker. He senses his conqueror. His reaction can take on various forms. In Mark 1:23 f and 5:7 he is already on the defensive. In Mark 1:23 f he begins with an outcry and uses defensive incantation formulas: "What have you to do with us, Jesus of Nazareth? Have you come to destroy us? I know who you are, the Holy One of God." The defensive formulation "what have you to do with us, Jesus of Nazareth?" is his attempt to disarm the opposition by naming his name. Something similar holds true for the term of phrase, "I know who you are. . . ." However, this demon speech quickly falls into a forced confession emphasizing Jesus' christological significance.

In Mark 5:7 we again have the beginnings of the demon's defense. The possessed person employs the same defense formula as in Mark 1:24. The following attempt to win power over Jesus by means of an incantation "I adjure you by God, do not torment me," does, to be sure, betray the demon's inferiority. He must recognize Jesus' power. In verse 9, when Jesus asks his name, there is a direct attack by the miracle worker, since the knowledge of the name serves to win power over the demon.

b) The actual exorcism in Mark 1:25 uses the command of silence as a part of the exorcism ritual which functions as a ban on the demon. Then follows the command to leave: "Come out of him!" In Mark 9:25 the command is extensively structured: "You dumb and deaf spirit, I command you, come out of him, and never enter him again." In exorcisms not dealing with Jesus as miracle worker, the exorcisms are effected by one's speaking the name of Jesus (Matt. 7:22; Mark 16:17; Acts 19:13).

c) The demons submit to the miracle worker's command, but only against their will. Thus, the retreat of the demon becomes a final attempt at employing force, and the possessed person's life becomes endangered by the unclean spirit's rebellion. The spirit convulses the sick person hither and yonder and leaves with a cry (Mark 1:26). The demon's final act of violence appears in a particularly graphic fashion in Mark 9:26. He cries out and tears the possessed person around so horribly that the narrator speaks of the following result: "And the boy was like a corpse; so that most of them said, 'He is dead.' " For this reason, a special healing by means of a transferral of power is necessary following the exorcism (v 27).

The final victory over the demon and its destructive power means the restoration of the sick person's own subjectivity. After the healing he then appears "in his right mind" (Mark 5:15) as opposed to the frenzy caused by the "unclean spirit" (5:3-4). The intervention of divine power itself is necessary to make this possible. The overcoming of the possession, the driving out of the demon, presupposes assistance that transcends the normal possibilities of the world. The original version of the narrative before the evangelist Mark already makes this clear (Mark 1:21-28). The spectators' reconstructed acclamation probably originally read as follows (1:27): "Who is *this one?* He commands the unclean spirits, and they obey him!"

Jesus is the subduer of demons, gifted with divine power (1:24). Mark 5:19 traces Jesus' exorcisms directly back to the mercy of the "Lord," namely, God. Liberation from demons is only possible as a miracle that breaks through existing boundaries and opens up the way of salvation.

2. The Understanding of Sickness and Healing in the Therapies

A miracle is to be designated as therapy when the demonological view of sickness only admits of an external demonic influence, and the healing is accordingly, not an exorcism of the unclean spirit, but rather a transferral of power. Attention should be paid to the fact that the sickness' demonological features—if at all—are preserved only in a faded form. Deafness and dumbness, for example, is considered to be a demonic "binding" of the tongue, and the healing a loosening of the same (Mark 7:35). In addition to the parallel in Luke 13:16, where the stooped condition is expressly designated as a "binding" by Satan, the documents from ancient binding magic also support the demonological understanding of the sickness as a "binding." The designation "disease" or "scourge" for the illness of the "hemorrhaging" woman might also ultimately go back to the image of a "demonic scourge" (Mark 5:29, 34; cf. PGM V 169 f). Fever is probably also traced back to demonic influence. Like a demon, it leaves Peter's mother-in-law (Mark 1:31). For the rest, however, demonological etiologies are missing from the New Testament therapy stories. This shows that they are not constitutive for the understanding of sickness found in the therapies.

How does the healing procedure appear in the therapies? Consider the portrayal in the story of the hemorrhaging woman (Mark 5:25-34). After bad experiences with physicians, the sick woman (an anomaly of the period?) directs her hope only to Jesus, whose reputation as a miracle worker has attracted her. Her expectation is that merely touching his garments is enough to heal her (v 28).

We find this view elsewhere as well: "And wherever he came, in villages, cities, or country, they laid the sick in the market places, and besought him that they might touch even the fringe of his garment" (Mark 6:56). Indeed, even handkerchiefs or aprons from the miracle worker (Paul) were thought to have healing power (Acts 19:12); even a shadow (of Peter) could work miracles (Acts 5:15). Behind this lies the belief in a power inherent in the miracle worker that flows from him as a kind of aura and is transferred to everything he touches. This flowing out occurs almost automatically, as the healing of the hemorrhaging woman shows. The woman acts in a way so that Jesus at first does not notice having been touched. Only when she is healed, after the power has gone over to the woman without conscious action on his part, does he notice it and ask: "Who touched my garments?" (v 30). The uniqueness of this story—a story thoroughly at home in the realm of Hellenistic thaumaturgy—

becomes particularly clear if one considers examples of Jewish healings of hemorrhaging. These are essentially characterized by two elements.[50] First there is a kind of folk-medical instruction, e.g.: "Let one take a handful of cumin, a handful of saffron and a handful of fenugreek, boil it in wine, and let her drink it. . . ." An order then follows: "Cease your discharge!" What is significantly missing is the idea of a power aura flowing from the healing person to the sick person and working on its own. New Testament miracle stories are also normally more reserved in this respect than Mark 5:25 ff. They speak otherwise about a plea for healing and Jesus' conscious laying on of hands for the purpose of a transferral of power, but not about the miracle worker's independent mana, which unfolds automatically. The massive borrowing of Hellenistic conceptions of power is, in Mark 5:25 ff, called forth by the special nature of the affliction, namely hemorrhaging. According to Jewish understanding, a hemorrhage made one cultically impure, and it forbade the sick person to come into the sanctuary or take part in religious festivals; indeed, it excluded them from human society like lepers. The rest of the Hellenistic world also considered touching a menstruating woman to be harmful. Because of the taboo associated with her illness, the hemorrhaging woman could not at all ask the miracle worker Jesus to heal her by the laying on of hands. She would have expected him to be contaminated. That is why she proceeds secretly (v 27) and is full of fear and trembling when she sees what has happened to her (v 33): She had, according to her own understanding, broken a taboo. On the basis of the story's conceptual presuppositions, a healing of the hemorrhaging woman could only come about by means of an illegitimate form of touch (by the woman herself). The Hellenistic understanding of power could be developed in a crass fashion, since it helped the healing to come about by means of (illegitimate) touching; the power—without Jesus' acting— flowed out to the woman of its own accord.

In the case of the hemorrhaging woman, the healing comes about by means of a transferral of power. The affliction is thus thought of as some sort of lack of vital power, if the miracle worker's power aura is able to mediate health. However, we need to caution against too extreme a conclusion here, since the idea of power in the first place only gets into the story with the figure of the miracle worker (the power is his unique possession) and only secondarily influences the understanding of the sickness itself. Nonetheless, the complex of power transferral, taken as a whole as a healing method, points to a corresponding understanding of sickness that is to be differentiated from that of the demonological interpretation, even if demonological motifs stand vaguely in the background (cf. Mark 5:29, 34).

In the other therapies as well, healing comes about by way of power transferral, above all, by means of touch (e.g., the laying on of hands). Even if there are examples of the laying on of hands in exorcisms in the early Christian surroundings, one hardly finds them in the New Testament. Touch heals fever (Mark 1:31), leprosy (Mark 1:41), hemorrhaging (Mark 5:27), speechlessness (Mark 7:33), blindness (Mark 8:22 f.), curvature of the spine (Luke 13:13), dropsy (Luke 14:4), and lameness (Acts 3:7). Indeed, along with the use of a healing statement, it even awakens the dead (Mark 5:41). In the healing of the hemorrhaging woman it was particularly clear that the purpose of touching included "strengthening the physically or spiritually weaker person."[51] Accordingly, we read in a summary remark of the evangelist Luke: "And all the crowd sought to touch him, for power came forth from him and healed them all" (Luke 6:19).

In the final analysis it makes no real difference "whether a deity lays its hand on the sick person or whether the sick person for his own part touches the deity in order to transfer healing power to himself through this contact."[52] It is always a matter of the mediation of powers, though in the New Testament the miracle worker Jesus usually takes the initiative.

In addition to touch, there are healing substances that mediate this power. We are speaking of the medicines designated as "powers," which the physician Erasistratos called the "hands of the gods." Thus a substance used against kidney stones is called a "hand of god" because of its superiority.[53] The only healing substance to appear in the New Testament is spittle;

in ancient folk medicine, blood, human breath, oil, or wine are used in addition. Breath and spittle are considered the mediators of special powers which these substances conduct from the power bearer to the sick person. Spittle, like blood, is particularly effective; it is "condensed breath" which comes out of the miracle worker. Spittle is employed for speechlessness when Jesus touches the dumb person's tongue with spittle (Mark 7:33), and for blindness when he spits directly into the sick person's eyes (Mark 8:23). In contrast to spittle salve, this gesture is more significant in exorcism ("a gesture of derogatory spitting"), and the actual mediation of power here occurs separately as a laying on of hands (Mark 8:23). Nonetheless, the association of the laying on of hands and spittle mediation in Mark 7:31 ff and 8:22 ff shows the related significance of both forms of power mediation. The fact that in 7:31 ff a healing statement is added (v 34; cf. also Mark 5:41) which for Greek ears would be a mysterious and thus magically powerful statement, changes nothing in the previous understanding of healing.

In the healing of the blind man in Bethsaida (Mark 8:22-26), Jesus' healing procedure is described more strongly in the analogy to a physician's method. After employing the first cure (spitting and the laying on of hands), Jesus asks the sick man about its effect (v 23). The blind man answers and can already register some success (v 24). Jesus then repeats the cure (the laying on of hands). The man is completely healed (v 25). In this healing procedure as well, Jesus remains the powerful miracle worker whose healing surpasses every normal activity of the physician. Again, it is the power dwelling in the miracle worker that goes over to the sick person and effects the healing.

Let us peripherally mention the healing of the man born blind in John 9:1 ff. Here, too, spittle serves as a healing substance. There is a complicated procedure in which Jesus spits on the ground and makes clay, which he then rubs on the man's eyes (v 6). The significance of the spittle is, of course, limited here, since the healing only succeeds after a washing in the pool of Siloam (v 7). In John 5:7 as well, it is presupposed that the water in the pool of Bethzatha (or Bethesda) contains healing powers "when the water is troubled" (movement caused by an intermittent spring?).

The demonstration of the therapeutic healing successes shows in conclusion that the healing consists in newly acquired power. The lame person is suddenly able to rise up, take up his pallet, and "go out before them all" (Mark 2:12), just as does the man awakened from the dead (Mark 5:42) or the blind man at the Bethzatha pool (John 5:9). The man with a speech impediment speaks correctly again (Mark 7:35). In the case of the blind man of Bethsaida (Mark 8:22-26), the healing is confirmed in stages. First the man goes about and only sees sketchily ("like trees"); after repeated laying on of hands he can see sharply and is fully restored (Mark 8:24 f).

Both motifs—healing as power mediation, as well as the demonstration of recovery in the sense of newly acquired power—reveal a particular view of sickness. "In the therapies . . . an understanding of sickness as weakness, or *astheneia,* gradually becomes visible which is different from the demonological etiologies of sickness."[54] The ill condition is viewed primarily as a power deficiency. The Greek word *astheneia* (actually meaning "weakness") for sickness may be mentioned in this context, even though its original significance in reference to the phenomenon of sickness is faded. In spite of this particular understanding of sickness in the therapies, in spite of the peculiar healing manipulations, in the final analysis we find the same understanding of overcoming sickness as in the exorcisms. The portrayal of the acclamations at the end of the stories betrays this. The healings are considered to be overwhelming miracles, behind which God himself stands (Mark 2:12); the means of healing correspond completely to those of other miracle workers: "So that they were all amazed and glorified God, saying, 'We never saw anything like this!' "

Just as everything God made during creation was good (Gen. 1:31), so also does Jesus' healing appear as a kind of new creation corresponding to God's own action (Mark 7:37). Jesus' activity is comprehensible for the narrators only as a sign of God's eschatological mercy towards his people (Luke 7:16).

3. Healing and Faith

After healing the hemorrhaging woman and the blind Bartimaeus, Jesus says the following: "Your faith has made you well" (Mark 5:34; 10:52). Modern scholars have used this sentence as an occasion to offer a one-sided psychological interpetation and to understand Jesus' healing methods as "psychotherapy." Accordingly all the sicknesses Jesus healed are interpreted psychogenetically, and are traced back to psychological disturbances. This not only holds true for the comprehensive phenomenon of possession, but also for paralysis, blindness, or deafness, which then appear as hysterical paralysis or functional blindness and deafness accessible to psychological influence. The sick person's faith is, then, the inner disposition first making healing possible at all. Jesus aroused faith and trust, but in so doing he also set a chain reaction in motion. "The overwhelming spiritual powers he set into motion unleashed the same powers of faith and will by way of psychological infection, including where they lay in unhealthy powerlessness."[55] The uniqueness of New Testament healings, that which separates them from magic, can be seen precisely in these psychologically determined healings rendered possible by faith.[56] This kind of explanation arises from modern-rationalistic concerns; they attempt to give a detailed analysis of the healing process enacted, and are supposed to illuminate the psychological mechanisms in terms of modern conceptions of causality. This does not, however, adequately take into consideration the uniqueness of these texts, which are to be interpreted within the framework of their own time. They do not allow us, without further ado, to bring our modern psychological categories into them. In any case, the evangelists knew nothing of considerations that viewed the healing process as the natural consequence of psychological influence. Healing was a *miracle*, possible only through the intervention of divine reality.

The concept of faith occurs in the context of ancient accounts of miracle healings. The purpose of the collection of miracle healings in Epidaurus is to give the sick hope and courage. In the face of the skepticism of many critics at that time, the faith, and thus also the will, for healing was to be strengthened. On the basis of individual miracle stories, we learn that the miracle was supposed to convert the unbeliever or skeptic so that he would trust the god's power.

In Epidaurus Miracle Number 3, a man unable to move the fingers of his hand comes as a supplicant to the god. However, when he sees the consecrated tablets in the sanctuary, he becomes unbelieving regarding the healings written down there. While sleeping in the holy room, he dreams that the god heals him. It asks him whether he is still unbelieving. He now answers, No. The healing thus made him believe. In Miracle Number 4, unbelief that considers the healings to be improbable and impossible, is called "ignorance," which the miracle overcomes.

Faith as the *result* of miraculous deeds has a parallel in early Christianity to the extent that miracles have an effect on the mission and awaken faith (Acts 9:42; cf. 19:17 f). The Gospel of John reports that Jesus' signs lead one to faith (2:11; 4:53; 10:41; 20:30 f).

More relevant, however, are the healing accounts in which faith is the *presupposition* of the miracle. A direct relationship between sickness and faith becomes visible here. In the situation of suffering, the sick person articulates an attitude that leads to an overcoming of the affliction. The attitude toward faith thus stands in direct relationship to the sickness. A clarification of what faith means here leads us to expect an illumination of the nature of sickness as well.

In ancient healing accounts this trust in the healing god is never called *pistis*, as it was in early Christian texts. Nonetheless, we do find a motif with the same substance, if not the same terminology. Epidaurus Miracle Number 37 relates about Aesculapius (the text is, to be sure, only a reconstructed one; cf. also Miracle 74): "The god will only heal those who come to him in his sanctuary in the good hope that he will do nothing to harm them, but will rather release them in good health." An extant epigram of the orator Aeschines offers an even more penetrating formulation[57]: "I was in distress as regards the arts of mortals, but I had all hope in the deity. . . . I was healed when I, O Aesculapius, came to your sanctuary. . . ." In the face of the failure of the medical arts, the sick person directs all his hope to the healing god, who does not disappoint him.

We find a similar situation in the story of the hemorrhaging woman (Mark 5:25-34). She had already suffered twelve years from her illness, and all the physicians' help had accomplished nothing. In the face of this experience of futility, she directs her entire trust to the miracle worker, Jesus (v 28): "If I touch even his garments, I shall be made well."

As in the case of the orator Aeschines, sickness that cannot be healed by human art is a threat to existence which, on the basis of its unbearableness, frees the hope in superhuman power and help as the last chance. There is, of course, a difference between the dimension of the sickness of the ancient rhetorician and that of the suffering woman. He suffered for one year from a head tumor; for over twelve years she was in a condition of perpetual "uncleanness," which for all practical purposes excluded her from human society. To her physical suffering was added the human isolation, which itself was associated with poverty because of the high but futile physicians' costs. In both cases, trust in superhuman power is an attitude of human existence that grows out of a situation of distress. This does not suggest that the expression of trust in the woman's soliloquy (v 28) is christologically determined in any exclusive fashion; it is not yet a matter here of faith in the miracle worker Jesus as the only Son of God. The woman is still alone in her experience of distress, but, at the same time, beyond it when by means of hope she transcends the situation of sickness and the limitation of human possibilities that goes with it. Faith is here a special manner of human existence, born in the experience of sickness and directed toward release from it. This interpretation is confirmed when we consider the substantiating statement at the end of the story: "Your faith has made you well" (Mark 5:34; cf. 10:52). It is emphatically the woman's faith that has brought liberation. This statement's function is worthy of notice. Jesus apparently only needs to confirm this healing faith. Normally, the miracle worker's statement is what first activates faith, so that healing can occur (Mark 5:36; 9:23; 10:49). Here, on the other hand, the woman's faith precedes Jesus' intervention. But even where the miracle workers's statement functions to awaken faith, this faith remains strictly related to the distress situation of sickness. The statement then stands in the context of a preceding plea to the miracle worker, characterized by an element of previous trust (Mark 9:22; 10:47).

The healing story in Acts 14:8 ff also speaks of this "miracle faith." Paul, as a miracle worker, only confirms "the faith to be made well" in a person crippled from birth. Faith here means the capacity to bring about a change in borderline cases in which a change appears totally impossible. This would include the hopeless situation of the woman who has suffered hemorrhaging for twelve years, the man crippled since birth (Acts 14:8 ff), and the father whose daughter is dying, and indeed dies during the course of the story (Mark 5:21-24, 35-43). The faith necessary for healing qualifies the sickness in a special way. Faith encounters man initially in a hopeless borderline situation, and any thought of the sickness' being overcome contradicts normal human expectation. Faith, however, frees the vision of the people in the miracle stories of what is actually impossible, namely the healing, and frees them to acquire it in trust.

We spoke of faith in miracles as a human attitude. It grows out of the distress situation in which the sick person has only this one hope left—a hope standing against all previous experience in life, in which serious illness leads to death. This confidence is despairing, paradoxical faith, just as the plea shows: "I believe; help my unbelief" (Mark 9:24). As much as it is a human attitude in which man goes beyond existing limits, to the same extent, however, it is possible only in the face of superhuman revelation encountered in the person of the miracle worker Jesus. His appearance in all the miracle stories provokes an expectation that mobilizes the sick person's energy to expect a fundamental change in spite of the borderline situation of sickness. It should be pointed out that nowhere is this faith called "faith in Christ" (or "faith in God," cf., however, Mark 11:22). The lack of such christological emphasis, which differentiates this conception from the Pauline concept of faith, shows that the narrators were concerned with the various human reactions to the epiphany of the miracle workers, reactions that, on the basis of their spontaneity, can do without any dogmatic concretization. Only after the successful healing do the miracle stories portray the spectators' acclamation, which itself formulates an extensive confession to Jesus (Mark 1:27; 7:37; Luke 7:16) or to God (Mark 2:12; 5:19).

Faith is, for the authors of the miracle stories, a gift, since it becomes a possibility for the sick person only through Jesus' appearance as a miracle worker. At the same time, however, it is an active faith, to the extent that it lifts the sick person out of the passivity into which sickness has forced him, an apparently unchangeable plight for a man in those times. The miracle worker's appearance and the expectation provoked by it arouse new activity. The man in need comes to Jesus (Mark 1:40; 5:25 f; Matt. 9:27), falls down before him (Mark 1:40), and expresses, in a plea for mercy (Mark 10:48; Luke 17:13; Matt. 9:27) and in a special expression of trust (e.g., Mark 7:28; 9:24; Matt. 8:8 ff; 9:28), his total willingness to receive everything from the miracle worker. This surrender appears to be the prerequisite for healing in the miracle stories. The sick person does not just let things go their own way, and does not just remain passive in order to let the miracle worker act. On the contrary, Jesus' mere appearance already activates his life spirit. The actual act of healing, however, remains for the miracle worker to perform.

The healing procedure comes about by means of a power transferral (touch or some healing substance)— or a command (in the exorcisms). These magically occurring healing methods appear to compete with the faith that heals. This is especially noticeable in Mark 5:25-34 and Mark 9:14-29. The hemorrhaging woman is liberated from her torment solely on the basis of the power of Jesus which flows over her (Mark 5:29). At the same time, however, Jesus states at the end of the story that her faith saved her (5:34). We find something similar in the exorcism in Mark 9:14 ff. First of all, the statement holds true that everything is possible for him who believes, meaning the trust of the person seeking aid (9:23). On the other hand, the exorcism of the unclean spirit comes about solely on the basis of the miracle worker's superior power (9:25 f). It might be possible to interpret this juxtaposition of motives in such a way that the magic healing method represents the traditional conception bound to the spiritual surroundings, a conception taken up by the narrator, but also corrected by the reference to saving faith. This interpretation is at least correct to the extent that the text in Mark 9:14 ff, in the oldest stratum in its tradition, contained a clear miracle, one of Jesus' thaumaturgical masterpieces. Now, however, on a new level of reflection, it introduces the problem complex of paradox faith. In the meantime: Do these two stories really deal with a corrective of magic conceptions? This does not appear to be the case when we consider that, each time, the healing method in question (power transferral or exorcism) is told with no deletions. It is not a matter of a corrective or even a suspension of magical presuppositions of thought, but rather of a deeper reflection bringing man's humanity more strongly into focus. The narrator is not satisfied simply with recounting the astonishing course of the healing; he lets the person seeking aid become transparent in his inner perspective. Thus we learn how the hemorrhaging woman experiences her own sickness and the healing procedure. Mark 5:27 reflects on the seriousness of the contaminating illness which drives the woman into human isolation, so that she only dares touch Jesus secretly, from behind. Verse 28, on the other hand, emphasizes the dimensions of her trust which contrast with the hopelessness of the illness: "If I touch even his garments, I shall be made well." Verse 33 then shows us the woman after the healing, still depressed because of the illegitimate nature of her behavior. Full of fear and trembling, she falls down before Jesus and admits secretly touching him, which touch has led to the healing. Verse 34, on the other hand, relieves the tension, because Jesus' statement declares the woman's faith, and thus also her behavior, to be in order. "Your faith has made you well." The illness has lost its enslaving inescapability, since, in the face of the revelation in Jesus, faith becomes a new power in the woman enabling her to overcome the illness.

The story of the healing of the possessed boy (Mark 9:14 ff) reveals the inner state of mind of the father seeking help, who pleads for his son. The destructive power of the sickness is so great here that the son himself can no longer plead, hope, or believe. But even the faith is initially capable of a despairing plea (v 22). Only Jesus' statement (v 23*b*) enables him to believe radically against all hopelessness associated with the possession, and against all previous experience of futility (cf. v 18): "All things are possible to him who believes." Nonetheless, this faith remains conscious of its own inner problems. It must believe and expect what is actually reserved only for divine omnipotence (v 23*b*). The human answer can thus only be (v 24): "I believe; help my unbelief!" In the miracle stories we have already seen in the Gospel of Mark, faith is already "prayer faith" in a preliminary fashion—namely, where it is expressed in the form of a plea. This can be seen, for example, when Jesus characterizes blind Bartimaeus' cry for help as faith: "Jesus, Son of David, have mercy on me!" (Mark 10:47 f and 10:52). In this sense Mark 11:24 can say explicitly: "Therefore I tell you, whatever you ask in prayer, believe that you have received it, and it will be yours."

The evangelist Matthew understands faith in a special way as prayer faith. Individual miracle stories are structured to serve the community paraenesis. They are to show the congregation in an admonishing and promising fashion that Jesus answered prayer in faith and will answer it again now, in the time of the church. This intention is expressed quite clearly in the formulations "Be it done for you as you have believed" (Matt. 8:13) or "Be it done for you as you desire" (Matt. 15:28).

The former turn of phrase is used in the story of the centurion of Capernaum. Here there is a clear correspondence between the centurion's plea (Matt. 8:8) and Jesus' answer to it (Matt. 8:13), where the centurion's supplicating posture is called faith. Jesus answers the supplicating faith and heals the sick servant. We find something similar with the Canaanite woman. To the woman's repeated cries for help which will not be quieted, Jesus finally answers: "Great is your faith! Be it done for you as you desire" (Matt. 15:28). In both stories the believing person is merely a supplicant, and there are extended conversations involving the pleas. These supplications stand for the prayer the evangelist wishes to commend to the congregation. This impression is strengthened even more because the centurion, as well as the Canaanite woman, appear in the role of intercessors representing others. The evangelist has understood both stories as examples for the congregation. In them they are to learn the significance of supplicating faith, i.e., prayer faith, for distressing situations. The same holds true for the portrayal of the healing of two blind men. Jesus answers their cry for mercy with the words: "According to your faith be it done to you" (Matt. 9:29). Members of the Christian community should, in a corresponding way, be certain their prayers will be answered.

4. Sickness and Sin, Healing and the Forgiveness of Sins

We have spoken until now about the distress of sickness, caused by its immediate physical and psychological destructiveness. It drove people into a hopeless situation where human aid failed. This experience of suffering could, however, be aggravated even more by the rejection coming from fellow men who considered the sickness to be a just punishment for alleged or real sins. Upon encountering a blind, lame, or leprous person, one was supposed to murmur: "Praise be the dependable judge!" (Tos. Ber. 7:3). It was too easy for the result to be self-righteousness, when a person was himself healthy and only asked about a sick neighbor's possible guilt instead of practicing solidarity in sympathy. The historical Jesus opposed the questionable consequences of this kind of requital thinking (Luke 13:1-5). What, then, was the attitude of the Christian communities?

We first have to consider that the dangerous implications of requital faith only represent one, the negative, side of the problem. However, in its own way, this thinking does justice to human experience in that sickness does not just mean physical damage, but also affects the whole person. Today, too, the religious dimension of sickness remains in view in the question concerning the sense or senselessness of sickness; at that time one tried to answer it with, Sickness is the consequence of sin. Actual healing of the sick person was thus not only a restoration of his physical well-being, but, in the New Testament, also aimed at the acceptance of the whole person by God. This is not, however, a pious denial of the terrible suffering brought about by sickness, a denial that sees only the actual affliction in man's sinfulness and disregards physical suffering. The story in Mark 2:1-12 shows just this, namely that the early Christian community viewed healing as a comprehensive phenomenon affecting man in his physical-spiritual, as well as religious, dimension.

Mark 2:1-12 relates the healing of a paralytic. A conversation about the power of the forgiveness of sins (vv 6-10) has already been added to an older miracle story (vv 1-5, 11-12) in the oral tradition. The statement concerning the forgiveness of sins in verse 5 probably provided the impulse for this thematic expansion. At first glance, Jesus' reaction to the faith of those bringing the paralytic to him appears astonishing. They are expecting the sick man to be healed, but he anwers them with the sentence: "My son, your sins are forgiven" (v 5).

This feature is also conspicuous in comparison with the other New Testament miracle stories, since the statement concerning the forgiveness of sins is missing there. There, the context of sin and sickness corresponds to Jewish tradition. Thus the Christian community also sees sickness as a reprisal for past sins. That is why the physical restoration of the sick person is not enough. Sickness is not just a physical problem here, but rather, in a comprehensive sense, an indication of the disturbed relationship to God. This comprehensive view of man and thus also of his illness makes a total change in his person necessary. That is why Jesus first tells the paralytic: "My son, your sins are forgiven" (Mark 2:5). This statement expresses the total acceptance of the person by God. The text allows Jesus to do justice to the Jewish principle: "The sick person will not arise from his sickness until one (i.e., God) has forgiven him all his sins" (Ned. 41a).[58]

Nonetheless, the statement concerning the forgiveness of sins is not the last word. This could, taken by itself, only be misunderstood as a religious consolation for the sick person that otherwise simply leaves him in his distress. Jesus thus utters the words of power that bring about the paralytic's bodily healing (v 11f). Both together, the forgiveness of sins and the healing of the sickness, represent the full restoration of the person. Rehabilitated before God and man, he returns to daily life (vv 11 f).

Behind the narrative in Mark 2:1-12 stands the Christian community; it is convinced of Jesus' power to forgive sins (v 10) and traces its own forgiveness procedure, which occurs through baptism, to him. The pardon of sins and the healing of the sick person belong together for them in the encounter with the complex phenomenon of sickness.

In the healing of the man blind from birth in John 9:1 ff, we find a slightly different attitude toward the theme of sickness and sin. There is a direct contradiction here of the Jewish belief in reprisal. A positive acceptance of this kind of thinking aiming at a comprehensive restitution of the sick person (as in Mark 2:1-12) is impossible in the face of the problem complex elicited by the story. Here, Jesus denies the existence of sin in the sick man or in his parents, a sin which might be the cause of his affliction (v 3). The reason for this attitude lies in the community's desire to ward off any tendencies more concerned with a self-righteous condemnation of the sick person than with aiding him. The disciples are not moved by the man's distress, but rather by the question of his possible guilt (v 2). They attempt to equate the sick person's sickness with sin and thus avoid the obligation to feel solidarity with him. The sick man is isolated, becomes an exception whose situation is his own fault, and departs from the company of the pious. The healthy person recognizes his undisturbed relationship to God in his good health; the sick person is caught in his sin. The healthy person's active concern for the sick thus becomes superfluous, and the sick person is left to himself and his suffering. In the face of such monstrous consequences for the belief in reprisal, only open contradiction is possible, and the community has Jesus express this (v 3). A productive acceptance of the view which sees a close relationship between sin and sickness and thus does justice to the comprehensive view of man, is impossible here in the face of the monstrous consequences of the reprisal faith.

In John 9:1 ff we probably find the post-Easter community speaking. Even if one reconstructs an earlier form of the present narrative, consisting perhaps of verses 1, 2, 3a, 6, and 7, one still cannot gain direct access to the historical Jesus. However, this state of affairs has only limited significance. John 9:1 condemns this kind of reprisal faith, which seduces one into self-righteousness and relieves one of any real responsibility; this reminds us of Jesus' opposition in Luke 13:1-5.

The attitude of the early Christian communities toward the relationship between sin and sickness was not a unified one. It varied according to the concrete problem requiring a solution. This kind of thinking could find positive acceptance if it served man's well-being (Mark 2:1 ff). It could be rejected if it distorted one's view of man's suffering (John 9:1 ff). Paul, too, reckons with the fundamental validity of this principle, without, to be sure, ever using it abstractly. Sick and weak people in the Corinthian community are an indication to him that the community has not done justice to the correct celebration of the Lord's supper (1 Cor. 11:30). Sickness and death appear as the terrible consequences. True, Paul does not accuse individual sick persons in the Corinthian community. That would be contrary to love. With an eye on these individual cases he warns the community as a whole of the dangerous consequences of their abuses, which even now are visible in the sicknesses and deaths.

5. Jesus Christ as Lord over Sickness in the Gospel Portrayals

It was a part of the view of the historical Jesus that his demon exorcisms were to demonstrate the advent of the kingdom of God. Satan, as the cause of misfortune and thus also of sickness, had to give in. God became Lord whenever Jesus had conquered a bastion of the demons (Luke 11:20). Jesus thought himself called to eliminate the demons and the sicknesses caused by them. The post-Easter community, in its fundamental inclination, did not think any differently, even though other conceptual associations became dominant (cf. the lack of eschatological interpretation of healings or exorcisms with the aid of the conception of the kingdom of God). In the miracle stories they showed Jesus as the one who had come to destroy the "unclean spirits" (Mark 1:24), who commands them and whom they obey (Mark 1:27). He shows himself to be the Son of God, of the Most High (Mark 5:7), as Lord over all corruptible uncleanness. In his activity one recognizes God's mercy (Mark 5:19). Indeed, just as of God himself, one can confess of him (Mark 7:37; cf. Gen. 1:31): "He has done all things well; he even makes the deaf hear and the dumb speak."

In their structuring of the Gospels, the evangelists reworked the miracle stories in their own way, stories originally told in another manner. They reinterpreted them within the framework of their own basic theological posture. Thus Mark took the miracle stories from the oral tradition and gave them new accents. The evangelist Matthew had the Gospel of Mark before him in written form and oriented his own Gospel according to it; he independently retold the miracle stories from Mark's Gospel and put his own views into them. In spite of this reworking, one motif appears again and again: Jesus proves his power and splendor precisely in the elimination of sickness. We will limit our own study to the evangelists Matthew and John, since their conception reveals this motif in particularly impressive fashion.

Matthew concentrates his presentation of the miracle stories in chapters 8 and 9 in the Gospel. Jesus appears here as the "Messiah of Action." With reference to his introductory remark concerning Jesus' healing activity in Matthew 4:23, he concludes his portrayal of Jesus' miracles with the following reference (Matt. 9:35): "And Jesus went about all the cities and villages, teaching in their synagogues and preaching the gospel of the kingdom, and healing every disease and every infirmity." And shortly before, Matthew has the crowd cry out the following, after the healing of a dumb person (Matt. 9:33): "Never was anything like this seen in Israel." He has the crowd ask about Jesus' significance (Matt. 12:23): "Can this be the Son of David?"

In Matthew, Jesus' miraculous deeds appear to be the powerful works of God's servant, as they are described in Isaiah 53:4. In a summary remark he thus determines Jesus' significance (Matt. 8:16 f): "That evening they brought to him many who were possessed with demons; and he cast out the spirits with a word, and healed all who were sick. This was to fulfil what was spoken by the prophet Isaiah, 'He took our infirmities and bore our diseases.' "

In what sense does Matthew understand the "bearing of our diseases"? In Isaiah 53 we encounter the servant as "a man of pains, and acquainted with sickness" (Isa. 53:3). The suffering servant is himself a sick person. His suffering, however, is a representative suffering, because "he was bruised for our iniquities; upon him was the chastisement that made us whole (Isa. 53:5). In this context, the statement of Isaiah 53:4, "he has borne our sicknesses and carried our pains," means that the suffering servant representatively bore and tolerated the diseases of others in himself.

Matthew did not understand the Old Testament passage in this sense. Jesus is not himself a sick person here, nor a representative sufferer. We encounter Jesus rather as the powerful master who, only as such, liberates the sick from their suffering. This is supported by the word-choice in which the Old Testament citation (Isa. 53:4) is formulated in an independent reproduction (against the original text): Jesus *took* and *carried* our infirmities, i.e., eliminated them. Out of the many passages concerning the suffering servant in Isaiah 53, Matthew takes only the one interesting him in order to interpret Jesus' miraculous healings: the "carrying or bearing of diseases" is only understood as the elimination of diseases, not as suffering itself.

Matthew portrays Christ in the miracle stories as the victorious Lord gifted with divine power who "brings justice to victory," as he says in a quotation from Isaiah 42:1-4 (Matt. 12:20).

At the same time, however, Christ is the "merciful." He himself desires mercy (Matt. 9:13). His healings are expressions of his mercy (Matt. 14:14; 20:34). With this conception in mind, the evangelist often uses the turn of phrase "have mercy" in the pleas in the miracle stories (Matt. 9:27; 15:22; 20:30, 31); in this, characteristically, the plea for mercy is followed by the address, "Son of David." The majestic master over all sickness is addressed, the master who removes it. Mercy and power are united in the person of Jesus.

In Matthew it is a matter of the healing of bodily sicknesses. Earthly life is taken seriously, and sickness has no figurative significance. Things are a bit different in the Gospel of John. In the story of the healing of the man born blind in John 9:1 ff, the evangelist took up a miracle account that originally included perhaps verse 1, 2, 3a, 6, and 7. In his reworking he introduces completely new aspects to the story. The disciples' question about who is at fault for the man's blindness, he or his parents, is rejected, and their focus is turned in a completely different direction. Jesus takes aim at the meaning and purpose of the blind man's suffering: God's salvation work is to be made manifest in this poor man (3b). This points toward the following healing by Jesus, the christological meaning of which is revealed. This is also the case with the illness of Lazarus (John 11:4): "This illness is not unto death; it is for the glory of God, so that the Son of God may be glorified by means of it."

The illness does not just become an opportunity to demonstrate Jesus' miraculous power; its healing opens up the view into deeper levels. It is a reference to the glorification of God who wants to realize the saving of the world in the sending of his Son (cf. John 3:16). This salvation aspect is expressly mentioned in John 9. During his stay on earth, Jesus is "the light of the world" (v 5). This refers to the fundamental self-revelation of the Son in John 8:12. The healing of the blind man thus has symbolic significance. Just as the blind man regains his eyesight, so also does faith receive the light of revelation from the Son of God. The Son's power does not merely manifest itself in individual healings, rather, it fulfills itself in his entire mission on earth which serves his glorification. For the faithful, however, it confirms that Jesus really is "the light of the world."

V. Paul's Illness

In Paul we find only a few allusions to sicknesses among the members of Christian communities (1 Cor. 11:30; Phil. 2:26 f).

The apostle treats this subject in relation to his own person. His own chronic affliction became a perpetual problem for him since it brought him hostility in the execution of his missionary office; indeed, it called into question the legitimacy of his proclamation.

We begin with Galatians 4:13-15. Paul is looking back at the first, the missionary visit to Galatia. Although at the same time the letter is being written the Galatians are threatening to fall away from the apostle because of the agitation of his opponents, they have not yet done him any wrong (v 12). In their initial meeting with him, however, they might have had reason to reject him. Paul reminds them that he preached the gospel to them though he was bodily sick (verbatim: "in sickness of the flesh," v 13). They did not, however, reject him for this (v 14): "And though my condition was a trial to you, you did not scorn or despise me, but received me as an angel of God, as Christ Jesus." The compressed and thus unclear manner of expression in the sentence's first part emerged from the admixture of two conceptions: "You did not scorn or despise me" and "And though my condition was a trial to you." If the first statement is still referring to the shameful, helpless condition in which the sick missionary encountered the Galatians, then in the second, the incomparably greater danger to his proclamation is expressed. Paul's illness could become a trial for the Galatians because it was pushing them to reject the person struck by sickness. Why? The illness was such that one could attribute it to demonic influence. The community did not perform the gesture warding off evil: spitting forth, something people in antiquity used against demonic danger of all kinds, and so also against the demonic influences of the sick; for example, epileptics and the insane. The Galatians overcame the fear of contamination and thus did not receive him as an angel of Satan, but rather as an angel of God, indeed, as Christ himself.

Two views of sickness appear to be juxtaposed here. Paul himself understands his sickness as a "weakness of the flesh," flesh meaning man's physical existence, specifically the body (also in 2 Cor. 12:7 in the phrase "thorn in the flesh"). This understanding also underlies the formulation in 1 Corinthians 11:30, where Paul speaks about "the weak and ill" in the community. In Greek both expressions used there imply a condition of weakness. The other possibility of interpreting his sickness is to explain it demonically. The apostle has just emphasized that the Galatians did not succumb to this temptation, which was very much suggested by his external appearance, his "flesh." We have already seen this double possibility of interpreting sickness in our investigation of the miracle stories. In the therapies we found the neutral view that understands sickness to be the absence of vital power. The exorcisms, on the other hand, were characterized by an unambiguous demonological understanding of sickness. Nonetheless, in the therapies we found that an exact determination of the various views of illness was difficult. There was apparently a transitional middle ground, and the sick person's external appearance could be interpreted in various ways. This is the case with Paul. Whereas he himself speaks only of a "weakness of the flesh," he had to reckon with the dangerous possibility of his affliction's being interpreted demonically, of his even appearing to be a possessed person and thus his message's being "satanized," or attributed to a demonic source.

One thing must, however, be taken into consideration. Even if Paul initially only speaks about the danger of a demonological misunderstanding of his affliction, we cannot exclude the possibility that the temptation lying in the apostle's "flesh" did not also appear to Paul himself to be caused by the "tempter," the devil (cf. 1 Thess. 3:5; 1 Cor. 7:5). The weakness associated with the sickness would then have been called forth by the devil in order to make his work more difficult. This would be paralleled by the suffering of the hemorrhaging woman (Mark 5:25 ff) or of the deaf and dumb person (Mark 7:31 ff), whose sickness primarily appears as the absence or lack of power, an absence which did not, however, come about without external demonic influence. The affliction is thus called a "scourge" ("disease" Mark 5:29, 34), or a "binding of the tongue" (Mark 7:35). This view would always be fundamentally differentiated from possession, since this demonic injury is limited and does not make the sick person into an involuntary object of the demon or of Satan. In Paul's case, this kind of "diagnosis" would make it clear why there was a danger the Galatians could misunderstand his sickness as possession. Its external appearance was ambiguous. His affliction could be based on a limited demonic influence, or it could represent a case of real possession. In 2 Corinthians 12:7 we then find the first interpretation. Paul traces his affliction expressly back to injuries inflicted by the messenger of Satan, and in Galatians 4:14 this kind of interpretation by the apostle himself cannot be dismissed too quickly.

In our investigation up to this point, we have tried to view Paul's sickness only with such categories as were within the apostle's own conceptual horizon. A diagnosis in the modern medical sense is problematic in view of the dearth of information given by the apostle. Again, in view of his friendly reception by the Galatians during his first missionary trip, Paul says (v 15): "For I bear you witness that, if possible, you would have plucked out your eyes and given them to me." One might understand this sentence to mean that Paul is employing the image of the eye as the most valuable thing man has in order to graphically indicate the Galatians' loving devotion. Another interpretation seems likely. The phrase, "if possible," speaks against the assumption of a merely proverbial manner of speaking. It disturbs the middle of the sentence, if one takes the sentence in a figurative sense. For this reason one might understand it literally and view the mention of eyes as an allusion to Paul's illness. If it had been possible, the Galatians would have given their own eyes in order to help the apostle's disturbed sight. Even if this interpretation is correct, we still have not found out very much about Paul's illness. A sight disorder alone would not have brought with it the danger that the Galatians would have rejected him because of demonic possession. More drastic, if possible even hideous, manifestations of sickness are necessary for that. The sight disorder was only an accompanying symptom of a more comprehensive condition.

We must now look at the second passage in which Paul speaks about his illness, 2 Corinthians 12:7-10. First of all, the context is important here. Paul does not speak about sickness as a problem of the Christian or even of man in general, but rather—just as in Galatians 4—as a threat to his apostolic office.

In the main section 2 Corinthians 10:12-12:18, Paul must explain his understanding of "boasting." He is forced to do this because of the behavior of his opponents, the so-called "superlative apostles," who base their own position on certain advantages they do not see in Paul, so that they challenge the legitimacy of his apostolate. He is forced into the situation where he must boast of such abilities and experiences which, according to his own understanding, should not be boasted of (12:1): "I must boast; there is nothing to be gained by it, but I will go on to visions and revelations of the Lord."

Because his opponents challenge Paul's apostolic authority with accusations of the absence of ecstatic experiences, he must speak of such pneumatic experiences in 2 Corinthians 12:1 ff. First, he reports an ecstatic elevation into the third heaven and into paradise; then, in the section of interest to us (12:7-10), he deals with a second revelation. The apostle explains. So that he would not become presumptuous like his opponents and use his ecstatic experiences as proof of his office, God gave him "a thorn in the flesh," which Paul identifies with the "messenger of Satan" who harasses him (v 7). This clearly refers to a physical affliction that continues in spite of repeated prayer (v 8) and thus seems to be a chronic illness. It is associated with significant pain, as Satan's harassment suggests ("blows of the fist"). Paul himself sees Satan's work in the affliction; in this he subscribes to the ancient demonological view which traces certain sicknesses back to "blows" by evil spirits.[59] To be sure, Paul does not follow this understanding so far that he sees the "blows" to be Satan's independent action. Satan is rather a tool of God, whose purposes he is to serve. The actual author of the affliction is God, as the circumlocution "a thorn was given me in the flesh" suggests.

Paul only gives very few references to the symptoms of his illness. He does not describe them for their own sake, but rather only within the context of theological disputes with his opponents. A medical diagnosis is made even more difficult because the manifestations of the sickness are expressed in the conceptual forms of ancient imagery ("blows of the messenger of Satan"). Nonetheless, a profusion of medical explanations have been attempted in scholarship, above all, epilepsy, serious hysteria, migraines, eye migraines (cf. the sight disorder mentioned in Galatians 4:13 f), and so on. Such interpretations, however, do not yield any firm results. It is thus understandable if one discounts such long-distance diagnoses of a patient who has already been dead nineteen hundred years. We will only briefly go into the diagnostic problem at this time. Instead of taking a position ourselves, let us consider the following citation:[60]

> Medically it seems most likely that, concerning Paul's having become ill [sic], we ought to think of endogenous depression. Being struck by the messenger of Satan can refer to the acutely occurring depressive change through which he is depressed, weak, and listless and suffers from strong, even physical feelings of disinclination. The often incomprehensible change in mood, the extraordinary activity, the strong self-consciousness, the rich, often volatile flow of thoughts in Paul during healthy periods all very much suggest a hyperthermic temperament which, as shown by experience, often induces periodic depression. The appearance of individual, ecstatic visionary conditions on this turf is not unusual, whereas epilepsy is improbable because of the nature of the basic temperament.

This diagnosis is based mainly on 2 Corinthians 12:7 ff, while Galatians 4:13 f is not mentioned. And indeed, the connection between the various suggested sight disorders in Galatians 4:13 f with the sickness meant by 2 Corinthians 12:7 ff does not appear to be so simple. The eye affliction would only be comprehensible as an accompanying manifestation of the more fundamental sickness (2 Cor. 12).

Paul's affliction is not the apostle's private, purely personal problem. Such an interpretation is excluded by the context in which he speaks of it. His explanation that the affliction was given him so that he not become presumptuous like his opponents and boast of his abilities, already excludes a purely individualistic interpretation. The problem of his sickness can be specified more precisely. The Corinthians knew of the "thorn in the flesh." For them it was probably an indication that Paul still remained caught in the realm of the "flesh" and did not belong to the "spiritual" realm (cf. 2 Cor. 10:2 f), as was required of a legitimate apostle. If one thinks of Galatians 4:13 f, then one will have to formulate the accusations even more sharply. The "thorn in the flesh" proved to his opponents that Paul was dominated by the messenger of Satan and was, to that extent, in a condition of "weakness," whereas they required "boasting" and "perfection" of an apostle. Paul takes up their objections and paradoxically turns them around: Indeed, he was suffering from the blows of the messenger of Satan, but this was given to him by God (v 7) so that he would not become presumptuous. If he did have to boast—as his opponents forced him to do through their agitation—then he would boast precisely of his "weakness" (2 Cor. 11:30; 12:5b, 9b, 10). Paul overcomes the temptation of his sickness by seeing in it the possibility that the power of the "Lord" is revealed in the face of his own suffering. The power of Christ shows itself in his weakness.

How is this overcoming of the problem of sickness to be understood more exactly? The text gives us an answer if we follow its thought sequence precisely. We should remain aware that Paul speaks of his affliction in a form characteristic of ancient accounts of "healing miracles."[61]

As regards style, 2 Corinthians 12:7 contains the description of the affliction. This is done by means of mythological categories of interpretation (the blows of Satan's angel), but not with expressions of ancient medicine.

In verse 8a Paul mentions his turn to the *kyrios*, as is typical in non-Christian healing miracles.

In verse 8b Paul cites the contents of his prayer to the *kyrios*. He "besought" the Lord, that the messenger should leave him.

In the non-Christian healing miracles the god then appears and the healing to be undertaken is revealed. Paul, too, seems to presuppose an appearance by Christ. It is, however, typical for him that he only reports a two-part statement by Christ (v 9a): "My grace is sufficient for you, for my power is made perfect in weakness."

This statement corresponds to the oracles that represent the divine (healing) answer in the context of the healing miracle. Whereas the god's statement is normally positive, there are examples showing a rejection of the plea. We find here a parallel to the rejection of healing in Paul's case. (v 9a).

An oracle can, for example, read as follows (Lucien, *Alexander* 28): "Spare the effort of seeking the cure for your sickness, *for* your fate is near, you cannot possibly escape it."

As other oracles show, these are variously structured in two parts. First, there is the actual manner in the form of an affirmation or a refusal of the same, and to this is added a kind of "theological statement" as a reason for it. This structure has been precisely maintained in Paul: "My grace is sufficient for you, for my power is made perfect in weakness."

The first line contains the refusal. His healing will not be granted. Christ refers rather to his "grace," which will be sufficient for the apostle. There is probably a word-play intended here with the word "grace." In ancient healing miracles "grace" *(charis)* means the divine healing power or deed. Paul would have been asking for Christ's healing act which would free him from his affliction. It is refused. Instead, Paul is referred to Christ's "grace" in a totally different sense. This suggests itself in the oracle's second line. It is a matter of the power of Christ which is made perfect in weakness. Christ himself was crucified in weakness, but lives from the power of God. For that reason—Paul says—we, too, are weak in him, but we will live with him by the power of God (2 Cor. 13:4). This hope, directed toward the future in 2 Corinthians 13:4, has significance for the sick apostle's present suffering. This hope reaches for the present and determines it. The "revelation of the life of Jesus" (2 Cor. 4:10) does not just happen in the future, but rather occurs already in the apostle's mortal body "under the mask of death." The future pulls the present into it, and for that reason Paul can write the paradoxical sentence: We are "as dying, and behold we live" (2 Cor. 6:9)—by means of the external power of God who has proven his power in the resurrection of Christ. The sickness remains what it is; suffering caused by the messenger of Satan. The apostle, however, is not cast to the ground by it, because he knows, on the basis of Christ's statement, that his, Christ's power really is enough for him (2 Cor. 12:9).

The oracle containing the rejection of his healing gives Paul an interpretation of his affliction within the framework of his apostolic existence. The apostle proclaims Christ as the Crucified One (Gal. 3:1, 1 Cor. 1:23; 2:2). His whole personal life, including his affliction, serves this proclamation task. His illness is a manifestation of weakness, and in that it corresponds to the existence of Christ, also weak in his suffering, but proceeding toward divine perfection. Paul continues to suffer under the "blows" of the messenger of Satan (cf. vv 7 ff). However, just as with his other weaknesses, his insults, hardships, persecutions, and calamities (2 Cor. 12:10), the sickness caused by the messenger of Satan is the place where the power of the crucified Christ is revealed.

After the healing oracle we normally find the confirmation of the healing, the offering of a sacrifice and the praise to the god. In Paul we only find the latter (v 9b): "I will all the more gladly boast of my weaknesses, that the power of Christ may rest upon me."

In conclusion Paul summarizes the experience he has gained from the sickness and the withholding of its healing: "For when I am weak, then I am strong." This sentence is not to be understood as general human knowledge; indeed it contradicts the basic human attitude. Paul comes to this paradoxical thesis only on the basis of the insight into the salvation event of Christ, who was crucified in weakness, but lives in the power of God (2 Cor. 13:4).

The experience of God's withholding the healing of sickness has found expression in several ancient texts. Important for our context are the documents in which the experience of lasting illness is assimilated inwardly. How could a Gentile contemporary of Paul accept physical suffering when, indeed, it meant a decisive limitation of earthly happiness?

Aelius Aristides, born in A.D. 117 in a city in Mycia, speaks about his long experience in dealing with serious illnesses. After the physicians had given up on him, he put his last hope in the god Aesculapius, and Aesculapius helped him. Aristides then became an ardent worshipper of his god, who in dreams continually gave him new instructions for healing his infirmities. In him we find a religious attitude toward sickness which, in comparison with Paul's attitude, can seem provocative.[62]

The election by his god is more valuable to Aristides, he says, than this mortal life. Neither sickness nor joy can change that. His god's direct turning to him gave him the will as well as the power to live. Aristides is willing to accept sickness if it accords with the god's will. When he suffers a series of bleedings during a cure in Pergamon (seat of a famous Aesculapian sanctuary), he answers the following to the physicians who suggest remedies: he is not master over his blood so that he can deal with it however it pleases him. Rather—as long as the god commands him to suffer the bleeding, he would obey whether he wanted to or not. Indeed, Aristides even goes so far as to explain that it is impossible for him not to desire it. The alternative between sickness or health no longer interests Aristides; what is important to him is the divine will and the immediate experience of his god. He is himself a person who has been able to live through many and various courses of life through the power of his god, and who thus virtually considers sickness to be advantageous. For this experience with the god he would not exchange that which among men is normally called happiness (Aristides, *Oration* 23:17).

Aristides experiences the help and daily instructions of his god. In spite of that, he does not become healthy. This is because he basically does not want to be healed. That would mean he could no longer experience his god's presence and proximity because he would no longer need him as a physician. And this is precisely what concerns him. In the final analysis it is not the problem of sickness or health that interests him, but rather the daily association with the god whom he believes he experiences again and again in his nightly dreams.[63]

We are dealing here with an extremely egocentric piety that takes on virtually neurotic features. It could thus have been prudent from the very beginning to avoid any comparison with Paul's attitude toward sickness. Nonetheless, there is a certain formal similarity in the piety structures. Both are decisively concerned with subordinating oneself to one's Lord and his will, and thus also to the distance that gives to one's sickness. The sickness is no longer an experience of insurmountable suffering, but is rather positively accepted through religiosity and put in a new horizon of meaning.

The differences in content in the two theologies are, however, more important than this formal similarity. Aesculapius promises his loyal adherents physical as well as spiritual aid. In Aristides this intimacy with the god is heightened to an exclusivity that excludes other reference points and only knows the ardent relationship between the worshipper and his god, and so can no longer see any really destructive power in sickness. Paul comes to a completely different position from the perspective of his christology. Christ is, for him, the one who, although rich, became poor *for our sake*, so that *we* would become rich through his poverty (2 Cor. 8:9). Paul understands his apostolic existence in the same way. He is not concerned with his own, merely egocentric experience with his Lord, but rather with the presentation of his apostolic life to the community so they can recognize the crucified Lord in him and in his proclamation. Just as Christ took suffering upon himself for men in order to reveal divine salvation, so also does the apostle carry Jesus' death in his body so that Jesus' life can also be revealed in his body (2 Cor. 4:10). His sickness is not a selfish means for him to obtain religious experience (it was for Aristides), but rather the opportunity—and here lies its only positive significance—to proclaim the power of the crucified Christ in his own existence.

For Aristides, sickness becomes the means he almost desires in order to experience the perpetually new attention of his god. He consciously withdraws from normal human experience, for which sickness is not the path to happiness, but rather to unhappiness. Here Paul appears to be thinking in a much more comprehensible fashion for us. In spite of its christological significance, sickness remains that which it had to be for men at that time: demonic-satanic injury whose seriousness he does not question. Paul does not jump over the earthly, distressful reality in some enthusiastic flight. He continues to take it seriously. Nonetheless, he sees his affliction in the light of the power of his crucified Lord (2 Cor. 4:8-10):

> We are afflicted in every way, but not crushed;
> perplexed, but not driven to despair;
> persecuted, but not forsaken;

struck down, but not destroyed;
always carrying in the body the death of Jesus,
so that the life of Jesus may also be manifested in our bodies.

Stoic philosophy deals with the overcoming of suffering in a particular way. The wise Stoic does not lose his inner freedom even in the most extreme hardships. The unpleasantries of existence appear to him only as *adiaphora* which do not affect him at a deeper level. Only false opinions and ideas torment men: "We indeed torment and limit ourselves; that is, our opinions place us in torment and narrowness" (Epictetus, *Dissertationes* I.25, 28). Paul, on the other hand, by no means tries to dispute the seriousness of his suffering in illness by means of some higher insight, or to negate it as a mere externality that does not affect the inner person. He does not just accept the affliction, but rather pleaded for its elimination (2 Cor. 12:8). Paul knows nothing of a withdrawal into inwardness, just as he rejects the moral appeal to his own powers. He knows himself to be supported by the power of Christ alone. The wise Stoic, in contrast, "stands upright under every burden . . . he knows his own powers and knows also that he was born to carry these burdens" (Seneca, *Letter* 71, 26). That is how he is able to disdain pain. The sick person is thus told: "Is it nothing when you bear sickness with self-control?" (Seneca, *Letter to Lucilius* 78). In the final analysis, this means that a person comes to terms with the fate allotted him, the fate he encounters as a "bitter medicine" (cf. Marcus Aurelius, *Meditations*, V. 8).

VI. Healings in the Early Church

Not only did Jesus heal the sick and drive out demons, the early church as a whole was a movement which turned its attention to the situation of the sick in a significant way. We already see this indirectly in the significance attributed to Jesus' miracle stories by the post-Easter community. These stories were transmitted not only because the community was convinced of Jesus' healing activity, but also because miraculous acts were a part of the Christians' reality after Easter. In its own miracles the community followed its master, who was the great model. The instructions to the disciples include the following (Luke 10:9; cf. Matt. 10:7 f): "Heal the sick in it and say to them, 'The kingdom of God has come near to you.' " According to this passage, Jesus' disciples are called to the same activity to which he was called. Here, too, we find an explicit ordering of the healings into the comprehensive event of the arrival of the kingdom of God. When the sick become well, that shows that God becomes Lord and that his salvation will is thus realized in this world. Nowhere else in the authentic words of the historical Jesus do we find this explicit association of healing and God's becoming Lord. Only the exorcisms appear as a decisive element in the coming kingdom of God (Luke 11:20). This could, however, just be an accidental impression resulting from the small documentary basis of Jesus' authentic words. The separately mentioned healings of Jesus in Matthew 11:5 are probably also understood as signs of the kingdom of God commencing in the present.

Later on, we no longer find the kind of eschatological interpretation of healing that is characteristic of the disciples' activity in Luke 10:9. The early church did not, on the whole, interpret its own healings as signs of the kingdom of God commencing now. When it speaks of Jesus' miracles (in the miracle stories), it does not mention this for Jesus' own understanding. When it reports its own exorcisms and healings, this motif is missing entirely. In his own version of the commissioning of the apostles, the evangelist Mark significantly passes over the kind of thinking still preserved in Luke 10:9 (Mark 3:14 f; 6:7). The accounts in Acts concerning the apostles' initial healings confirm this picture (Acts 3:1 ff; 5:12 ff; 8:7; 9:32 ff, 36 ff).

Jesus had driven out the demons "with the finger of God" (Luke 11:20). Easter caused the disciples to change their focus; Jesus became for them the heavenly "Son of Man," the Son of God (cf. Rom. 1:4). Now they drove out demons and healed the sick "in the name of the Lord," i.e., by calling on the name of Christ and in his power (cf. Matt. 7:22; Luke 10:17; Acts 3:6, 4:7, 10; 19:13). They were conscious of not doing this "by their own power" (Acts 3:12). Accordingly, Peter says the following to the bedridden Aeneas, who has been paralyzed for eight years: "Jesus Christ heals you" (Acts 9:34). Even though, in part, a relatively late tradition is being expressed in the Acts account, it nonetheless accurately portrays the early Christian conviction: Jesus Christ gives the community the power to perform its own miracles.

This conviction concerning the power given the community to heal sicknesses could, to be sure, give rise to serious temptation. The early Christians had to experience bitterly that this miraculous power was not always simply at their disposal. Their attempts to heal the sick and drive out demons could fall short. We find a reflection of this experience in Mark 9:14-29, projected, to be sure, back into the situation of Jesus' disciples. The possessed child's father complains about the disciples' unsuccessful attempts to drive out the demon (v 18). At the end of the story, after Jesus himself performs the exorcism, the problem is taken up once again. The disciples ask Jesus: "Why could we not cast it out?" (v 28). Jesus answers (v 29): "This kind cannot be driven out by anything but prayer." The characterization "this kind" shows that the case at hand was particularly serious. According to widespread tradition, only prayer can help here (Acts 9:40; 28:8; James 5:15). What is meant here is the miracle worker's exorcism prayer, known also in Judaism where such psalms as Psalm 3 and Psalm 91 were considered to be "highly effective exorcism means." This prayer is missing in the preceding story. The "spirit" is driven out on the basis of the father's faith (vv 22-24) through Jesus' power statement in verse 25. However, the narrator probably inserted his own ideas into an already existing narrative context.

Faith and prayer are the fundamental prerequisites of miraculous deeds (Mark 11:23 ff). This is also shown by the fact that, in the miracle stories dealing with Jesus, the miracle always occurs as the fulfillment of a previously uttered plea (expressed as a petition or in the form of some act). In the final analysis this is the conviction that only the plea or prayer of the person seeking help makes the healing possible. The petition articulates that person's trust and faith in the miracle worker: "If you will, you can make me clean" (Mark 1:40).

The evangelist Matthew particularly emphasized the relationship between faith and miraculous healing, between petition and miracle. Two stories are characteristic here, in which the person seeking aid does not plead for himself, but rather for another (Matt. 8:5-13; 15:21-28). Here the believer is a supplicant from the very beginning, or more precisely: he is an intercessor representing another person. The necessary relationship between faith, which expresses itself in a petition, and the healing is spoken in a formal fashion: "Be it done for you as you have believed" (Matt. 8:13). "Be it done for you as you desire" (Matt. 15:28).

Basically, however, it is the situation of the supplicant who believes in the miracle worker that is shown by the fact that Jesus' statements follow extended plea conversations in which the intercessor describes the distress in the place of the person suffering, expresses his faith and pleads for help. Faith is here "prayer faith," which corresponds to the early Christian conviction concerning the prerequisites of prayer and faith for healing. Hence, Jesus can say the following to the two blind men, on the basis of the plea for mercy and the following confession of faith: "According to your faith be it done to you" (Matt. 9:29).

In the last-mentioned passage we spoke about the faith or prayer of the person seeking aid; in Mark 9:28 f, however, we spoke about the indispensable prayer of the person wanting to perform a miracle. According to the context of the statement concerned one or the other is emphasized. Paul speaks, self-evidently, about the faith that moves mountains (1 Cor. 13:2). This is referring to that faith that can help the community perform miracles (cf. Mark 11:23; Matt. 17:20). Accordingly, in a long series listing the community's various gifts of grace, Paul discusses the particular charisma of "faith" (1 Cor. 12:8-10): "To one is given through the Spirit the utterance of wisdom . . . to another faith by the same Spirit, to another gifts of healing by the one Spirit, to another the working of miracles. . . ." The context makes it clear that "faith" here is one gift among others. It means the capacity to perform miracles, as suggested by the immediate proximity of the healing gifts and miracle activities. It is not the faith common to all Christians, but rather a particular charisma given only to a few Christians for the purpose of healing. Apparently there were miracle workers in the community who had the task of healing or of manifestations of power. The differentiation between "healing gifts" and "miracle workings" as two different gifts of grace might point to the juxtaposition of healings (of the sick) and the actual exorcisms; we also encounter these separated as therapies and exorcisms in the Gospel miracle stories.

In Paul this gift of healing and of exorcism is given to those distinguished by special spiritual possessions (cf. the emphasis on spirit in 1 Cor. 12:8-10). Things developed later in such a way that these charismata were institutionally bound, and were considered the tasks of certain ecclesiastical office bearers. According to the Letter of James, the "presbyters," or church elders, have the task, among others, of healing the sick (James 5:14 f): "Is any among you sick? Let him call for the elders of the church, and let them pray over him, anointing him with oil in the name of the Lord; and the prayer of faith will save the sick man, and the Lord will raise him up; and if he has committed sins, he will be forgiven." This admonition proceeds according to the principle that sickness is a malady (cf. also James 5:13) and as such is not simply to be tolerated stoically, but should rather be eliminated. The elders' prayer and the anointing with oil are to make the sick person well again. In this emphasis on the prayer necessary for healing, the author is following the already well-known early Christian tradition, and is also following it by associating the prayer with the miracle worker's "faith." The anointing with oil of the sick person does not mean the same thing here as did extreme unction later during the Middle Ages, since the anointing with oil served to heal the sick person, not to prepare him for death. Here, as in Mark 6:13 and Luke 10:34, oil as a substance of folk medicine acquires a therapeutic function. It serves as a means of power transferral for the sick person. It is unlikely that this anointing is understood as part of an exorcism during which the sickness demon is driven out "by calling on the name of the Lord." The anointing "in the name of the Lord" is hardly to be interpreted as meaning that Christ's name is used here as a word of power against a demon. More likely is the more general assumption that prayer and anointing with oil occur by commission, in the name, and in the power of the Lord. Neither the prayer, nor the oil, nor the name of the Lord spoken by the miracle worker work magically or automatically here, because the author expressly emphasizes that the Lord himself will lift the fallen one. The elders' prayer and anointing with oil have a service function in the healing, which in the final analysis goes back to the Lord.

The text considers the possibility that past sins are the cause of the sickness. The forgiveness of sins mentioned after the healing (5:15) already suggests this. The following admonition, however, especially presupposes that successful healing includes a confession of sins and prayer. Sin as the basis of sickness must be eliminated (James 5:16): "Therefore confess your sins to one another, and pray for one another, that you may be healed."

Biblical Concern with Sickness as a Theological Problem: Encounters

1. The biblical writings are not really interested in sickness as such, but rather in the existential experiences associated with sickness. They portray the distress of sickness, the physical suffering as well as the social consequences resulting in the isolation from famliar company (e.g., as in leprosy). They speak, above all, about healing as the overcoming of suffering. They almost completely lack any objective, scientific interest which would be the prerequisite for considering sickness as a purely medical problem or as the isolated result of certain organic processes. That is why it is so difficult to say from which sickness this or that person seeking aid suffered in individual cases. These texts do not satisfy the scientifically oriented interest of the

modern reader. They do not deal so much with sickness as with being sick.

The differentiation between sickness and being sick plays a significant role today in psychosomatic medicine, which has set the distress of sickness as the criterion for being sick. The essence of sickness is distress, which expresses itself in the plea for help. Attention is no longer directed only to the scientific abstraction, sickness, but rather to the sick person as well. An understanding of sickness that only deals with the personally indifferent organic and physiological processes, scorns, in the final analysis, the concrete person and his suffering. A view, however, that considers the subjectively experienced distress of sickness, the psychological experiential world of the sick person, and his individual history, has a greater chance of doing justice to him and thus also of healing him.

An interpreter of biblical texts will recognize a concern in psychosomatic medicine that is comparable to the basic inclination of the biblical concern with sickness. No doubt there are fundamental differences between the two areas; indeed they lie on different levels, to the extent that the one is concerned with scientific reflection on sickness and the other with testimonies of faith emerging from being directly affected by the distress. This difference does not, however, prevent us from seeing what is common. The whole person comes into view; sickness is seen as a phenomenon of suffering with various dimensions, representing both a physical as well as spiritual event and, in its complexity, eliciting the question of meaning.

2. Then, as today, sickness was seen as a threatening fate. As distress, it could be experienced as a break in one's previous life history, as fated misfortune, or as an irrational fate. The question concerning meaning then arises. "This question of meaning," however, "presupposes resignation and the loss of meaning. The meaning capable of making the suffering bearable appears to be hidden."[1] In the biblical writings we encounter various attempts to give an answer to this question of meaning. If the sickness is traced back to the activity of gods and demons, then there is an attempt to explain the horror of sickness in a mythically rational fashion in order to get a hold on what is

actually unexplainable. There is also the possibility of fighting the sickness with the aid of a healing anti-power. If the sickness is taken to be punishment for past guilt, this interpretation signals the presence of a particular understanding of the nature of health. Health is not only bodily wholeness, but also involves a person's moral integrity, his accountability before God and man. Sickness appears to indicate a disturbance transcending a person's physical condition. In spite of the positive aspect of such religious interpretations of meaning, their consequences are not innocuous. If the demonological understanding of the world, and thus also of sickness, gains the upper hand, then there exists the threat that the world in general will be demonized. Sickness as punishment for past sins, on the other hand, easily seduces one into condemning the sick person and forgetting the necessary solidarity with his suffering. The biblical authors often do know of such religious interpretations of meaning, but we also find them attempting to get beyond it. The Book of Job is theologically the most significant attempt in the Old Testament. In the New Testament these religious interpretations are, for Jesus or Paul, only the presuppositions they find before them. They follow the various interpretations of sickness, but overcome them by putting the distress of sickness into a new, more comprehensive field of meaning.

"Jesus does not convince the sick and possessed that their sickness has a particular meaning; he just heals them, as the miracle accounts show, of their affliction."[2] That is no doubt correct. However, Jesus can cast out the demons and heal the sick only because he himself comes from a new experience of reality and meaning, namely, the inbreaking kingdom of God. For Jesus, healing is not just newly acquired health, but rather the end of the power of both Satan and death, and only to that extent, the end of the power of sickness.

Another objection goes as follows: "It is the danger of every religious interpretation of the meaning of sickness that it helps the sick person integrate the sickness into his own life framework, but at the price of forcing him at the same time to capitulate to the sickness."[3] This can be the case if the sickness appears to be willed by God, or as God's test or punishment for past guilt. There can easily be a resigned adaptation to the sickness, which appears to have a right to the sick person precisely because it is associated with God. On the other hand, the biblical writings (above all, the New Testament), indeed show that sickness does have power over the sick person, but no right to him. God stands against sickness, not with it! The texts do, to be sure, show that each healing occurs within the framework of a new understanding of meaning that has its own religious components.

3. In view of the new interpretation of the meaning of sickness in the New Testament, we cannot overlook the difference obtaining in this respect between the Old and New Testament texts. In their fundamental views, both parts of the canon appear to be similarly disposed, since they see the phenomenon of sickness within the framework of faith only as a part and sign of the relationship with God. The psalm prayers, as well as the theological confessions, document this: e.g., "I am Yahweh, who alone heals you," as does the Book of Job in the Old Testament. For the New Testament, Jesus' proclamation of the kingdom of God and Paul's self-understanding are firm proof. To this extent the New Testament gives the early Christian community an unambiguous answer to the fourth question posed above (OT IV.6.): The *solus* Christ is, in a new form, the fundamental element in every dealing with sickness. This line succeeds in maintaining itself. Concerning the three other problems not solved in the Old Testament, we can say the following from the New Testament perspective: The social question (1), particularly recognizable in the distress of the psalmists, is emphatically taken up in early Christianity (James 5:14-16; 1 Cor. 12:9 f). Medicine (2), in its contemporary form, remains for the most part outside the field of view for the Christ faith. This faith, however, facilitated the individual's and community's adoption of a sovereign attitude (3) toward suffering and sickness; neither death nor life could pull it away from trust in God's love (Rom. 8:35 ff). Jesus' proclamation of the inbreaking kingdom of God, the community's faith in the power of the Son of God over sickness and death, as well as Paul's conviction concerning the power of the crucified Christ are, each

in its own way, testimonies of the human experience of meaning signaling a new way of coming to terms with distress and sickness.

4. Jesus carries on his struggle against possession and other sicknesses under the sign of the proclamation of the kingdom of God. He did not attempt to give categories of meaning to the sick enabling them to bear the affliction more easily. Rather, he knew himself to be called to eliminate sickness and the powers standing behind it. Sickness contradicts the salvation will of the creator God, who wants life and not death. That is why Jesus wanted to save the concrete person in his life, i.e., strengthen and maintain him, and not to kill a human life by omitting the helping act (cf. Mark 3:4). His acts occur in an emphatically religious context of meaning. They spring from faith in God, who now finally comes to power and reestablishes the salvation of his creation. This religious aspect does not give Jesus occasion to preach surrender to sickness, but rather provokes his resistance to it.

As documents of the early Christian community, the New Testament miracle stories follow this inclination. Nowhere do we find the admonition to tolerate sickness and to come to terms with it; the exorcisms are concerned rather with the struggle against anti-divine powers in general, and the therapies are concerned with the mediation of a new power that makes healthy life possible. And wherever the attempt is made to interpret the meaning traditionally (in the question concerning the sick person's or parent's possible guilt), Jesus turns it away (John 9:3). For their own part, the gospel writers portray Jesus as Lord over sickness. As the prophesied suffering servant of the Old Testament, he "takes" the afflictions and "bears away" our diseases (Matt. 8:17). God and his Son are glorified in the face of sickness and healing; sickness is not "to death," but rather serves to realize the all-encompassing work of salvation (John 11:4). The evangelist John does not intend to integrate sickness and suffering as an other-worldly dispensation, intervening in life as we know it, but rather to understand the healing of sickness as a symbol showing that God and the Son of God want to "glorify" themselves by the saving of the faithful. On the basis of this

biblical document one will probably conclude: "A theology
oriented toward this gospel is concerned with an interpretation
of the meaning of sickness only to the extent that it helps the sick
person come to terms both internally and externally with the
sickness."[4]

5. The statement, "The meaning of sickness is to overcome
it," is biblically grounded as a principle of pastoral care.[5] On the
one hand, it means that the healing of the sick person and the
restoration of his health correspond to God's salvation will for the
world. On the other hand, it means that sickness does not have
any right to the sick person, so that he must not despair or be
resigned even in the case of an incurable illness. From this
perspective, pastoral care of the sick will first have the task of
strengthening the will to live. Above all, Karl Barth represented
this position. According to him, sickness cannot be traced back to
God; it is "like death itself, unnatural and disorderly, an element
in the rebellion of chaos against God's creation, and an act and
declaration of the devil and demons."[6] In sickness there is thus a
contrary power that one is permitted only to reject or protest.
But this is only one aspect. Pastoral care will also follow the goal
of leading the sick person to the sovereign freedom of faith. This
position corresponds to Paul's remarks concerning his own
affliction. This goal is important to the extent that it is a matter of
an incurable chronic illness. The question arises, however,
whether pastoral care that only intends to mediate opposition to
sickness does not collapse in the case of someone who is incurably
ill. Here one needs to speak about that special freedom Paul
learns in the face of his own affliction. The refusal of healing
demands that Paul accept his weakness. This acceptance,
however, is not a capitulation. It means only that he recognizes
his weakness. Paul belongs to Christ: "My grace is sufficient for
you" (2 Cor. 12:9). Regarding Paul, who is incurably sick, this
statement means that in this case as well, the meaning of sickness
lies in overcoming or coming to terms with it. On a purely
physical level sickness maintains its power, yet Paul behaves in a
way showing his freedom from sickness.

Considered psychologically, he goes through a kind of
maturation process. In his repeated prayers to the Lord he works

against sickness. This is the attempt at an assimilation characterized by opposition. Paul, however, does not remain in this protest position, but gets beyond it. The Lord's statement in 2 Corinthians 12:9 signals the insight leading to a new identity. The symbol of the crucified Christ who now, however, lives in power, makes the personal change possible. He conforms to this Christ and knows himself to be supported by the power of God active in Christ. Sickness has lost its enslaving power. It is overcome even if it continues to exist in its physical facticity (cf. Rom. 8:35 ff). His acceptance of suffering is not resignation, but rather marks a new focus finding its basis in Christ.

6. In contrast to the Old Testament, the New Testament offers us no extensive lament of a sick person who rises up against sickness and articulates his impatience, his despair, and his protest. The Old Testament supplicant asks why he is suffering and how long the hardship will go on. The accusation against God emerges from the lament of the distress. But here, too, he does not fall away from God, but argues rather on God's terms and appeals to his mercy. In the laments there develops an activity that fights against any resigned acceptance to suffering and struggles free from the oppressive paralysis of dull suffering. Paul's three-fold prayer asking the Lord to heal his affliction (2 Cor. 12:8) can be considered a New Testament analogy. The particular aspect of lament, however, is not addressed. We should, however, pay attention to that particular activity aroused in the sick in the miracle stories when they hear of Jesus' nearness. They come, plead for help, and appeal to the miracle worker. To be sure, this plea hardly takes on the form of lament or accusation as in the psalms, but carries within it rather a strong element of trust in the miracle worker: "Jesus, Son of David, have mercy on me" (Mark 10:48; Luke 17:13). We encounter the objecting lament only in the saving miracle in Mark 4:35 ff: "Teacher, do you not care if we perish?" (v 38). In spite of the absence of lament which expresses opposition to sickness, the activity and initiative Jesus provokes is important. The sick person no longer remains in hopeless passivity, but rather awakens to new vitality when Jesus the miracle worker comes near. Not only does the healing itself express the will to live in

the miracle stories, the sick person's initiative does so as well. The sick person's lament is absent because the miracle stories are characterized by the certainty of the present, effective healing power of Jesus.

7. If pastoral care of the sick sees its goal as strengthening the will to live, it will have to consider that it will encounter limitations. There is also the extreme case of the incurably sick person who really does not want to live anymore; in the face of this kind of suffering one cannot force the will to live on such a person: "The pastoral counselor, finding himself in this concrete situation, has to respect the person's will to death. For the sake of the freedom about which the gospel speaks, he also has to free the person for death."[7] The New Testament does not discuss this case directly. However, Paul considers the possibility that in the face of his distressful captivity, and in the face of the prospect of being with Christ after death, death would be a gain for him. Paul decides in favor of life so that he can further serve the community through his proclamation (Phil. 1:21-24). Nonetheless, death comes into view here as a positive possibility. The fact, however, that Paul finally decides in favor of this life and not of death, shows clearly that the will of death would be the extreme case. Otherwise, the preservation of life is a higher priority.

Notes

A. Old Testament

1. Cf. K. Menninger, *Das Leben als Balance. Seelische Gesundheit und Krankheit im Lebensprozess* (1968); A. Mitscherlich, T. Brocher, O. von Mering, K. Horn (editors), *Der Kranke in der modernen Gessellschaft*, Neue wissenschaftliche Bibliothek, Nr. 22: Soziologie (1967); A. Mitscherlich, *Krankheit als Konflikt. Studien zur psychosomatischen Medizin I und II*, edition suhrkamp 164, p. 237 (5th ed. 1969; 4th ed. 1969); G. Ruhbach (editor), *Krankheit und Tod*, Bethel Beiträge, vol. 9 (1973); H. Schipperges, *Porträt des Kranken und der Krankheit in Medizin und Philosophie*, Universitas 2 (1975); I. Illich, *Medical Nemesis. Die Enteignung der Gesundheit* (1975); E. Gerstenberger, W. Schrage, *Leiden*, BK 1004 (1977).

2. K. E. Rothschuh (editor), *Was ist Krankheit? Erscheinung, Erklärung, Sinngebung*, Wege der Forschung CCCLXII (1975); same author, *Der Krankheitsbegrif (Was ist Krankheit?)*, Hippokrates 43 (1972), pp. 3-17 (ibid. pp. 397-420).

3. Ibid., p. 414.

4. Cf. M. Josuttis, "Zur Frage nach dem Sinn der Krankheit," WzM 27 (1975), pp. 12-25; C. Westermann, "Heilung und Heil in der Gemeinde aus der Sicht des Alten Testaments," ibid. pp. 1-12; M. von Rad (editor), *Anthropologie als Thema von psychosomatischer Medizin und Theologie*, UT 607 (1974).

5. Concerning this topic cf. W. Ebstein, *Die Medizin im Alten Testament* (1901, reprinted 1965); A. Lods, "Les idées des Israélites sur la maladie, ses causes et ses remèdes," in: Marti-FS, BZAW 41 (1925), pp. 181-93; L. Köhler, *Der hebräische Mensch* (1953, reprinted 1976); J. Scharbert, *Der Schmerz im Alten Testament*, BBB 8 (1955); J. Hempel, *Heilung als Symbol und Wirklichkeit im biblischen Schrifttum*, NAWG I (1958/3, 2nd ed. 1965); A. R. Johnson, *The Vitality of the Individual in the Thought of Ancient Israel*,

2nd ed. (1964); P. Humbert, "Maladie et médecine dans l'Ancien Testament," RHPhR 44 (1964), pp. 1-29; Th. Struys, *Ziekte en Genezing in het Oude Testament* (1968).

6. Cf. K. Seybold, *Das Gebet des Kranken im Alten Testament. Untersuchungen zur Bestimmung und Zuordnung der Krankheits- und Heilungspsalmen*, BWANT 99 (1973), pp. 19 ff; same author, article "*hālāh*," ThWAT II (1976), pp. 960-71.

7. Ibid., pp. 961 ff.

8. J. F. A. Sawyer, "A note on the etymology of *sara ' at*," VT 26 (1976), pp. 241-45.

9. J. J. M. Roberts, "The Hand of Jahweh," VT 21 (1971), pp. 244-51.

10. K. Seybold, op. cit., pp. 48 ff.

11. Cf. E. Neufeld, "Hygiene Conditions in Ancient Israel (Iron Age)," BA 34,2 (1971), pp. 42-66; H. Weippert, "Bad und Baden," BRL (2nd edition 1977), pp. 30 ff; then W. Th. Im der Smitten, "Patient und Arzt. Die Welt des Kranken im Alten Testament," Janus 61 (1974), pp. 103-129.

12. W. Schrank, *Babylonische Sühnriten besonders mit Rücksicht auf Priester und Büsser*, LSemSt III, 1(1908, reprinted 1968), pp. 62 ff.

13. K. Seybold, op. cit., pp. 56 ff; 77 ff.

14. G. E. Wright, *Biblische Archäologie* (1958), pp. 166 f; cf. BHHW III, part 52. Cf. W. Ebstein, op. cit.

15. H. W. Wolff, *Anthropologie des Alten Testaments* (1973), pp. 21 ff; 96 ff.

16. Chr. Barth, *Die Errettung vom Tode in den individuellen Klage- und Dankliedern des Alten Testamentes* (1947); K. Seybold, op. cit., pp. 31 ff.

17. About 17 kilometers northwest of Jerusalem.

18. Cf. O. Keel, *Die Welt der altorientalischen Bildsymbolik und das Alte Testament. Am Beispiel der Psalmen*, 2nd ed. (1977), pp. 73 f; RTA ATD Erg. 1 (1975), pp. 264 ff.

19. Ug VI (1969), pp. 393 ff.

20. H. Gese, *Die Religionen Altsyriens*, Religionen der menschheit 10,2 (1970), pp. 141 ff; D. Conrad, "Der Gott Reschef," ZAW 83 (1971), pp. 157-83.

21. J. Gray, *The Canaanites* (1964), p. 123.
22. ANET pp. 148 f.
23. M. Dietrich, O. Loretz, J. Sanmartin, "Bericht über ein Orakel" (RS 24.272 = Ug.5, S. 563 Nr.6), UF 7 (1975), pp. 540 f.
24. EA Nr. 137.
25. EA Nr. 49.
26. A. P. Léca, *La médecine égyptienne* (1971), pp. 120 f; O. Keel, op. cit., p. 177, reproductions 270, 270a.
27. A. L. Oppenheim, *Ancient Mesopotamia. Portrait of a Dead Civilization* (1964); E. K. Ritter, "Magical-Expert (Āšipu) and Physician (Asû): Notes on Two Complementary Professions in Babylonian Medicine," in: Landsberger-FS, Assyriological Studies 16 (1965), pp. 299-321.
28. E. Ebeling, *Aus dem Tagewerk eines assyrischen Zauberpriesters*, Mitteilungen der altoriental. Gesellschaft V, 3 (1931, reprinted 1972).
29. K. Frank, *Babylonische Beschwörungsreliefs*, LSemSt III, 3 (1908, reprinted 1968) A; Text pp. 36 ff; O. Keel, op. cit. Nr 91, T. IV, pp. 68 ff.
30. AOB Nr. 387; ANEP Nr. 658; O. Keel, op. cit. Nr. 91/92.
31. According to E. Ebeling AOT, pp. 133 f.
32. S. N. Kramer, *Sumerian Mythology*, 2nd ed. (1961), p. 71; Th. Jacobsen, "The Cosmos as a State," in: H. and H. A. Frankfort, *The Intellectual Adventure of Ancient Man* (1967), pp. 161 ff.
33. O. R. Gurney, *The Tale of the Poor Man of Nippur*, Anatolian Studies 6 (1956), pp. 154-64.
34. C. Burde, *Hethitische medizinische Texte*, Studien zu den Boğazköy-Texten 19 (1974).
35. D. Brandenburg, *Priesterärzte und Heilkunst im alten Persien. Medizinisches bei Zarathustra und im Königsbuch der Firdausi* (1969).
36. E. Brunner-Traut, *Die alten Ägypter. Verborgenes Leben unter Pharaonen* (1974), p. 156.
37. Ibid., p. 160.
38. H. Grapow, *Kranker, Krankheiten und Arzt. Vom gesunden und kranken Ägypter, von den Krankheiten, vom Arzt und*

von der ärztlichen Tätigkeit. Grundriss der Midizin der alten Ägypter III (1956).

39. W. Westendorf, *Papyrus Edwin Smith. Ein medizinisches Lehrbuch aus dem alten Ägypten* (1966), pp. 21 f.

40. E. Brunner-Traut, op. cit., p. 147.

41. E. Edel, "Ägyptische Ärzte und ägyptische Medizin am hethitischen Königshof. Neue Funde von Keilschriftbriefen Ramses' II. aus Boğazköy," Rhein.-Westfäl. Akademie der Wissenchaften. Vorträge G 205 (1976), pp. 53 ff.

42. A. Erman, "Der Brief eines Kranken an seinen Sohn," in: Amtl. Berichte aus den Preuss. Staatssammlungen, XL 3 (1918); E. Brunner-Traut, op. cit., p. 152.

43. O. Temkin in: H. Flashar (editor), *Antike Medizin*, WdF 221 (1971).

44. Cf. A. Dupont-Sommer, "Exorcismes et guérisons dans les écrites de Qoumran," VTS 7 (1960), pp. 246-61.

45. *Das Formgeheimnis der biblischen Erzählungen, Kleinere Schriften* (1937), p. 139, cited according to: *Wenn die Götter schweigen* (1963), p. 210.

46. Cf. subsequent reference in 2 Kings 18:4.

47. Cf. 2 Sam 12; 13; 24.

48. Cf. here the beautiful Egyptian illustration in O. Keel, op. cit., Nr. 270, p. 177.

49. H.-P. Müller, "Die weisheitlische Lehrerzählung im Alten Testament und seiner Umwelt," WdO 9/1 (1977), pp. 77-98.

50. G. Fohrer, "Überlieferung und Wandlung der Hioblegende," in: Baumgärtel-FS (1959), pp. 41-62 (Studien zum Buche Hiob [1963], pp. 44-67).

51. W. von Soden, "Fischgalle als Heilmittel für die Augen," AfO 21 (1966), pp. 81 f.

52. G. Bornkamm, "Lobpreis, Bekenntnis und Opfer," in: APOPHORETA, Haenchen-FS, BZNW 30 (1964), pp. 46-83 (Geschichte und Glaube I, Gesammelte Aufsätze 3 [1968], pp. 122-39).

53. A. Erman, "Denksteine aus der thebanischen Gräberstadt," SAB 1911, pp. 1086-1110; E. Brunner-Traut, op. cit., pp. 145 ff.

54. Translation according to W. W. Hallo, "Individual Prayer in Sumerian: The Continuity of a Tradition," AOS 53 (= JAOS 88/1 [1968]), Essays in Memory of E. A. Speiser, pp. 82 ff (71-89).

55. Further reading: S. Mowinckel, *Psalmenstudien I-VI*, SNVAO (1921-24, 2nd ed. 1966); H. Schmidt, "Das Gebet der Angeklagten im Alten Testament," BZAW 49 (1928); Chr. Barth, *Die Errettung vom Tode in den individuellen Klage- und Dankliedern des Alten Testamentes* (1947); F. Michaeli, "Les malades et le Temple dans l'Ancien Testament," Église et Théologie 21 (1958), pp. 3-12; R. Martin-Achard, "La Prière des malades dans le psautier d'Israël," Lumière et Vie 86/17 (1968), pp. 25-43 (Approche de Psaumes, CTh 60 [1969], pp. 49-65); L. Delekat, *Asylie und Schutzorakel am Zionheiligtum. Eine Untersuchung zu den privaten Feindpsalmen* (1967); O. Keel, "Feinde und Gottesleugner," SBM 7 (1969); W. Beyerlin, *Die Rettung der Bedrängten in den Feindpsalmen der Einzelnen auf institutionelle Zusammenhänge untersucht*, FRLANT 99 (1970); E. Gerstenberger, "Der bittende Mensch. Bittritual und Klagelied des einzelnen im Alten Testament," Hab. Heidelberg 1971; same author, "Der klagende Mensch. Anmerkungen zu den Klagegattungen in Israel," in: Probleme biblischer Theologie, von Rad-FS (1971), pp. 64-72; H. Goeke, "Das Menschenbild der individuellen Klagelieder. Ein Beitrag zu einer alttestamentlichen Anthropologie," Diss. Bonn 1971.

56. Chr. Barth, op. cit.

57. J. A. Sanders, "The Psalms Scroll of Qumrân Cave 11 (11 QPsª)," DJD IV (1965); same author, "Two Non-Canonical Psalms in 11 QPsuª," ZAW 76 (1964), pp. 57-75.

58. Translation according to Seybold, op.cit. pp. 188 ff.

59. Cf. G. von Rad, *Wisdom in Israel* (1970).

60. H. Gese, *Lehre und Wirklichkeit in der alten Weisheit. Studien zu den Sprüchen Salomos und zu dem Buche Hiob* (1958).

61. Translation (German) according to the Einheitsübersetzung

der Heiligen Schrift, Kath. Bibelanstalt (1974). English according to RSV.

62. J. C. de Moor, "Rāpi'ūma-Rephaim," ZAW 88 (1976), pp. 336 ff.

63. J. Hempel, " 'Ich bin der Herr, dein Arzt' (Ex. 15:26)," ThLZ 82 (1957), pp. 809-826; same author, "Heilung als Symbol und Wirklichkeit im biblischen Schrifttum," NAWG I (1958/3, 2nd ed. 1965).

64. Reproduction from O. Keel Nr 90a, p. 68.

65. E. V. Hulse, "The Nature of Biblical 'Leprosy'—and the Use of Alternative Medical Terms in Modern Translations of the Bible," PEQ 107 (1975), pp. 87-105.

66. S. G. Browne, Leprosy in the Bible, 2nd ed. (1974), pp. 18 ff; E. V. Hulse, op. cit., p. 89; cf. L. Köhler, "Aussatz," ZAW 67 (1955), pp. 290 ff.

67. J. F. A. Sawyer, "A note on the etymology of ṣara ' at," VT 26 (1976), pp. 241-45.

68. In E. V. Hulse, op. cit., pp. 97, 98.

69. M. Noth, Das dritte Buch Mose. Leviticus, ATD 6 (1962), p. 89.

70. Cf. K. Elliger, Leviticus, HAT I 4 (1966).

71. This is the opinion of M. Noth.

72. This is the opinion of E. V. Hulse.

73. Concerning the behavioral patterns in 13:45 f., cf. K. Seybold, op. cit., pp. 49 ff.

74. M. Noth, op. cit., pp. 89 ff.

75. J. T. Ingram, "The significance and management of psoriasis," British Medical Journal II (1954), p. 823, translated according to E. V. Hulse (German), op. cit., p. 100.

76. R. de Vaux, Das Alte Testament und seine Lebensordnungen, Vol. 1 (1960), pp. 111 ff.

77. W. F. Kümmel, "Melancholie und die Macht der Musik. Die Krankheit König Sauls in der historischen Diskussion," Med. hist. Journal, Hildesheim 4 (1969), pp. 189-209.

78. In: K. Schneider-FS. Arbeiten zur Psychiatrie, Neurologie und ihren Grenzgebieten (1947), pp. 77-85.

79. A. Klostermann, "Ezechiel. Ein Beitrag zu besserer

Würdigung seiner Person und seiner Schrift," ThStKr 50 (1877), pp. 391-439.

80. E. C. Broome, "Ezechiel's Abnormal Personality," JBL 65 (1946), pp. 277-92.

81. W. Zimmerli, *Ezechiel*, BK 13 (1969), pp. 26 ff.

82. Concerning 3:26 f, cf. W. Zimmerli, op. cit., note p. 30; R. R. Wilson, "An Interpretation of Ezekiel's dumbness," VT 22 (1972), pp. 91-104.

83. E. Vogt, "Die Lähmung und Stummheit des Propheten Ezechiel," in: Wort—Gebot—Glaube, Eichrodt-FS, AThANT 59 (1970), pp. 87-100.

84. H. D. Preuss, *Deuterojesaja. Eine Einführung in seine Botschaft* (1976).

85. K. Baltzer, "Zur formgeschichtlichen Bestimmung der Texte vom Gottesknecht im Deutero-Jesaja-Buch," in: Probleme biblischer Theologie, von Rad-FS (1971), pp. 27-43.

86. Article "*hālāh*," ThWAT II (1976), pp. 967 f.

87. H.-P. Müller, "Ein Vorschlag zu Jes 53:10 f," ZAW 81 (1969), pp. 377-80.

88. W. Zimmerli, "Zur Vorgeschichte von Jes LIII," VTS 17 (1969), pp. 236-44 (Studien zur alttestamentlichen Theologie und Prophetie. Gesammelte Aufsätze II, ThB 51 [1974], pp. 213-221); E. Kutsch, *Sein Leiden und Tod—unser Heil. Eine Exegese von Jesaja 52:13—53:12*, BSt 52 (1967).

89. F. Horst, *Hiob 1*, BK 14/1 (1968), pp. 26 f.

90. Arabia Petraea III (1908), p. 413, cited from F. Horst (German), op. cit., p. 27.

91. Cf. Isa. 40:2.

92. A. Alt, "Zur Vorgeschichte des Buches Hiob," ZAW 55 (1957), pp.265-68.

93. C. Westermann, *Der Aufbau des Buches Hiob*, CTM 6, 2nd ed. (1977).

94. G. Fohrer, *Hiob*, KAT, 2nd ed. (1963).

95. F. Horst, op. cit., p. 64.

96. F. Horst, op. cit. (from the German). English according to RSV.

97. Cf. H.-P. Müller, "Altes und Neues zum Buch Hiob," EvTh 37 (1977), pp. 284-304.
98. G. Hölscher, *Das Buch Hiob*, HAT I 17, 2nd ed. (1952). English according to RSV.
99. E. Ruprecht, "Die Religion der Väter. Hauptlinien der Forschungsgeschichte," DBAT 11 (1976), pp. 28 ff.
100. J. C. de Moor, "Rāpi'ūma—Rephaim," ZAW 88 (1976), pp. 323-45.
101. *Vom Geist der Ebräischen Poesie* (1782) I,V.

B. New Testament

1. Cf. L. Edelstein, *Der hippokratische Eid*, ed. H. Diller, Zürich 1969.
2. Ps. Hippokrates, De morbis I 6.
3. O. Temkin, "Griechische Medizin als Wissenschaft und Handwerk," in: Antike Medizin, ed. H. Flashar, Wege der Forschung CCXXI (1971), p. 17 (1-28).
4. J. Schumacher, *Antike Medizin, Vol. 1: Die naturphiloso-phischen Grundlagen der Medizin in der grieschischen Antike* (1940), pp. 179 ff.
5. H. E. Sigerist, "Die historische Betrachtung der Medizin," Archiv f. Geschichte d. Medizin 13 (1926), p. 18 (1-19).
5. H. E. Sigerist, "Die historische Betrachtung der Medizin," Archiv f. Geschichte d. Medizin 13 (1926), p. 18 (1-19).
6. Cf. R. Herzog, *Die Wunderheilungen von Epidauros* (1931).
7. Op. cit., p. 60.
8. Op. cit., p. 66.
9. Op. cit., p. 75.
10. Op. cit., p. 76.
11. Op. cit., p. 148.
12. E. and L. Edelstein, *Asclepius. A Collection and Interpretation of the Testimonies II* (Baltimore: 1945), p. 154.
13. Ph. Derchain, "Die ägyptische Welt nach Alexander dem Grossen," in: *Der Hellenismus und der Aufstieg Roms. Die Mittelmeerwelt im Altertum* II, Fischer Weltgeschichte 6 (Frankfurt: 1965), p. 243.

14. Cf. the edition by K. Preisendanz, *Papyri Graecae Magicae*, 2 vols (1928).
15. G. Theissen, *Urchristliche Wundergeschichten*, StNT 8 (1974), p. 240.
16. Translation (German) according to V. Hamp, *Sirach* (1951), Echter-Bibel. English according to RSV.
17. In the reconstruction in A. Schalit, *König Herodes*, Studia Judaica IV (1969), pp. 638 f.
18. H. Strack/P Billerbeck, *Kommentar zum Neuen Testament aus Talmud und Midrasch*, Vol. IV, 1 (1969 = 1928), pp. 504 f.
19. Op. cit., Vol. IV, 1, p. 532.
20. Op. cit., Vol. II, p. 529.
21. Op. cit., Vol. I, pp. 444 f.
22. Op. cit., Vol. II, pp. 196 f.
23. Op. cit., Vol. I, p. 495.
24. Op. cit., Vol. II, p. 441.
25. Cf. J. Becker, *Johannes der Täufer und Jesus von Nazareth*, Biblische Studien 63 (1972), pp. 71-85.
26. J. Jeremias, *Neutestamentliche Theologie, Erster Teil: Die Verkündigung Jesu* (1971), p. 96.
27. German translation and interpretation according to G. Dautzenberg, "Sein Leben bewahren. Psyche in den Herrenworten der Evangelien," StANT 14 (1966), pp. 154 f; R. Pesch, *Das Markusevangelium*, HThK II, 1.Teil (1976), pp. 192 f. English according to RSV.
28. According to H. Strack/P. Billerbeck, op. cit., Vol. I, p. 750.
29. R. and M. Hengel, "Die Heilungen Jesu und medizinisches Denken," in: Medicus Viator, Festg. f. R. Siebeck (1959), p. 341 (331-361).
30. R. Pesch, "Jesu ureigene Taten?", Quaestiones Disputatae 52 (1970), pp. 140 f.
31. W. E. Mühlmann, *Chiliasmus und Nativismus* (1961), p. 252.
32. H. Strack/P. Billerbeck, op. cit., Vol. I, p. 491.
33. G. Bornkamm, "Pneuma alalon," in: same author, *Geschichte und Glaube* 2. Teil, BevTh 53 (1971), pp. 24, 28 f.
34. Cf. E. Lesky/J. H. Waszink, RAC V, pp. 819-831.

35. E. Lesky, RAC V, pp. 829 f.
36. E. V. Hulse, "The Nature of Biblical 'Leprosy' and the Use of Alternative Medical Terms in Modern Translations of the Bible," Palestine Exploration Quarterly 106/107 (1974-1975), p. 88.
37. F. W. Bayer, article: "Aussatz," RAC I, p. 1023.
38. H. Strack/P. Billerbeck, op. cit., Vol. IV, p. 751.
39. Op. cit., Vol. IV, p. 751.
40. Op. cit., Vol. IV, p. 751.
41. R. Pesch, "Jesu ureigene Taten?," op. cit., p. 79.
42. Cf. W. Schrage, ThDNT VIII, pp. 270 ff.
43. H. Strack/P. Billerbeck, op. cit., Vol. I, p. 525.
44. Citations in W. Schrage, ThDNT VIII, p. 282.
45. W. Schrage, ThDNT VIII, p. 284.
46. F. Fenner, Die Krankheit im Neuen Testament, Untersuchungen zum Neuen Testament 18 (1930), pp. 70 f.
47. R. Herzog, op. cit., pp. 98 f.
48. F. Fenner, op. cit., p. 61.
49. G. Theissen, op. cit., p. 94 ff.
50. H. Strack/P. Billerbeck, op. cit., Vol I, p. 520.
51. H. Waagenvoort, article: "Contactus," RAC III, p. 405.
52. O. Weinreich, Antike Heilungswunder, Religionsgeschichtliche Versuche und Vorarbeiten 8 (1909), p. 63.
53. Op. cit., p. 37.
54. G. Theissen, op. cit., pp. 72, 101.
55. F. Fenner, op. cit., p. 95.
56. Op. cit., p. 94.
57. R. Herzog, op. cit., p. 39.
58. H. Strack/P. Billerbeck, op. cit., Vol. I, p. 495.
59. O. Weinreich, op. cit., pp. 59 f.
60. K. Bonhoeffer in H. Lietzmann, An die Korinther I/II, HNT 9, 4th ed. (1949), p. 157.
61. H. D. Betz, "Eine Christus-Aretalogie bei Paulus (2 Cor. 12:7-10)," ZThK 66 (1969), pp. 288 ff.
62. Concerning the following cf. A.–J. Festugière, Personal Religion Among the Greeks (Berkley/Los Angeles: 1960), pp. 96, 100.
63. Op. cit., p. 86.

Biblical Concern with Sickness

1. F. Wintzer, "Sinn und Erfahrung. Probleme und Wege der Krankenseelsorge," in: Theologie und Wirklichkeit, Festschr. f. W. Trillhaas, ed. H. W. Schütte and F. Wintzer (1974), p. 221.
2. M. Josuttis, *Zur Frage nach dem Sinn der Krankheit*, Wege zum Menschen 27 (1975), p. 14; similarly H.-Chr. Piper, *Kranksein—Erleben und Lernen*, Beratungsreihe 4 (1974), p. 31.
3. M. Josuttis, op. cit., p. 15.
4. Op. cit., p. 14.
5. Op. cit., p. 15.
6. K. Barth, Church Dogmatics III/4, p. 366.
7. M. Josuttis, *Praxis des Evangeliums zwischen Politik und Religion* (1974), p. 139.